RED TO BLACK
IN 30 DAYS

D1565196

RED TO BLACK IN 30 DAYS

An Accountant's Guide to *Quick*
Small Business Turnarounds

Allen B. Bostrom, CPA

Published by
Universal Accounting Center
12441 S 900 E
Draper, UT 84020

Books are available for business or quantity discounts.
Telephone the publisher at 800.343.4827.

Printed in the United States of America

ISBN 978-0-9764702-1-2

CONTENTS

vii **ACKNOWLEDGMENTS**

ix **FOREWORD**

1 **PART I – DISCOVER – What is going on here?**

1 Introduction – Making a difference

14 Chapter One – Being a profit expert

38 Chapter Two – Setting up the project

66 **PART II – Develop – What needs to be done?**

67 Chapter Three – Step 1 – Assessing the situation

97 Chapter Four – Step 2 – Planning the turnaround project

127 Chapter Five – Step 3 – Improving cash management

144 Chapter Six – Step 4 – Reducing expenses

161 Chapter Seven – Step 5 – Increasing revenue

181 Chapter Eight – Step 6 – Monitoring and Reassessing

202 **PART III – DOCUMENT – What did you learn?**

202 Chapter Nine – It's working! Now you are an expert.

ACKNOWLEDGMENTS

Our mission here at Universal Accounting Center is to provide accounting-based products and services that maximize organizational profitability and individual effectiveness. I am dedicated to that mission and *Red to Black in 30 Days* complements both those initiatives.

I want to thank my colleagues at Universal Accounting Center who live and breathe that mission. I thank them for their dedication, hard work, for their ideas and support that went into this book and for their never-ending passion for success of small businesses everywhere.

Our clients and students at Universal Accounting are the center of our work universe. They made great suggestions for this book and have enthusiastically supported its completion. I greatly appreciate their contributions.

I acknowledge the work of a great friend and associate, Scott Stephenson, without whom this book would have never happened. His support and valuable experience have made him a key resource in *Red to Black* concepts and principles.

Thanks go to my father, Alf Bostrom, who instilled in me a love for business and a desire to help others be successful.

And a great thank you to my wife Sheri who has been a tremendous encouragement and support throughout my career.

Thank you to all.

FOREWORD

This book shows you how to grow your accounting practice, make more money and gain expertise in helping troubled small businesses—making them profitable once and for all. It is a guide to *quick* small business turnarounds.

You know small business owners; they have a never-ending supply of problems. Some problems are serious and some are not, but they are always there. The problems are rarely anticipated and sometimes, these business owners cannot see the problems right before their very eyes.

Then, all of a sudden, there is not enough cash to last through the end of the month or even through the end of the week! Or maybe expenses are out-of-control. Or sales drop unexpectedly. Desperation sets in quickly.

Where do these small business owners turn for help?

Usually their accountants gets the first visit—if they have one. If *you* are the accountant, you may be the only person in a position to help turn the business around and become profitable! You can be the business owner's *Profit Expert*—or turnaround expert.

As a Profit Expert, you can advise the business owner as to what he can do right now to make the business more profitable. This book can be your coach if you do not currently have that expertise!

The book is divided into three parts: **DISCOVER, DEVELOP,** and **DOCUMENT.** The three parts follow a continuous improvement model that can be applied to all aspects of the business.

PART I—DISCOVER—sets the stage for how small business accountants can help in business turnaround situations—turnarounds that need to be made right now, not in six months or even 90 days.

Even 60 days may seem like an eternity. Some actions need to be taken immediately. The next 30 days are critical!

Our tendency is to rush too quickly into action. You want to *do* something the first day that will help the business recover. However, before you do anything, you need to discover what is going on in your own practice and in your business relationship with the business owner. The turnaround project needs to be set up correctly so that you and the business owner can each reach your goals. Then you can proceed to the **DEVELOP** phase.

PART II—DEVELOP—outlines the six action steps in the turnaround process. The book provides the models, processes, and monitoring tools necessary for developing and implementing a turnaround plan.

The six action steps work. The process starts with an assessment that will enable you to formulate a plan to navigate those activities that are easiest to control within the business. The process progresses through marketing and building revenue. Reassessment is done at the end of this section to see what progress has been made and what still needs to be done. When this work is done, one major phase remains:

PART III—DOCUMENT—captures the major learning points from the turnaround process for the business owner specifically regarding his own business. Then the accountant can focus on what he learned that can help in the growth of his own accounting practice.

You don't *have* to follow this process; you can try something else if you want. But this process works.

Is this the answer to every problem?

Probably not! Not all small businesses can be turned around, and not all of them in 30 days. But if a business can be turned around, the process and tools presented in this book will help!

Read on. You'll find many answers here.

INTRODUCTION
Making a Difference

Your accounting practice is steady or growing slowly. You want it to grow more quickly, with more and better clients, more revenue and more challenging projects. Some of your small business clients have big problems and you may feel uncomfortable or inadequate to help them. You need a coach yourself or a guidebook you can use to help you deal with small business clients that are in trouble. *Red to Black in 30 Days* is your guidebook.

YOU CAN MAKE A DIFFERENCE

As the accountant, you may be the first one to see and understand that the business is either having trouble or headed for trouble. The information from the financial statements can be life-saving when communicated to business owners in a timely fashion. You have the responsibility to tell business owners there are major problems if you know about them.

This communication can be a real wake-up call to the business owner. But there is hope. You can help; remember, you want to be associated with these businesses for the long term.

The models and processes outlined in this book will become second nature to you. This expertise will allow you to expand or even specialize your accounting practice in business turnarounds. If you are an internal accountant, *Red to Black in 30 Days* provides strategies and tactics that can make you much more valuable within your organization.

YOU CAN MAKE MORE MONEY

Of course, you need to be compensated for your work. That might be your biggest problem. How do you collect payment if the businesses you work for are struggling? *Red to Black in 30 Days* will help you with that as well.

Instead of charging clients for monthly or quarterly compilations of accounting information, you can charge them for your work as a trusted advisor and turnaround consultant.

Perhaps most importantly, the processes and models outlined in this book enable you to expand your accounting practice and make more money. Expertise in business turnaround strategies will increase the value of your services, and you can charge your clients accordingly.

You can prove your value as an accountant, the value of accounting information and gain a reputation as a profit and growth expert. Perhaps, for compensation, you can earn a small monthly commission and a percentage of future profits. If the business is currently losing money, the business owner will experience little or no risk in giving you a percentage of future profits. He will be better off than he is right now—and so will you.

MY OBJECTIVE FOR WRITING THIS BOOK

Here are two reasons why I wrote this book:

First, accounting students, clients, small business owners and small business accountants ask me many questions. The question I hear the most is:

How can I help a small business owner turn around his business quickly—like right now, not in months, but in a matter of days or weeks?

This book addresses that question by outlining a process that will work for any small business.

The second reason I wrote this book is because the first book I wrote *(In the BLACK—Nine Principles to Make Your Business Profitable)* focused on how to *make* and *keep* your business profitable. It did not address ways for turning a business around—making a profitable business out of one that might be headed for closure in perhaps a matter of days or weeks. *Red to Black in 30 Days* answers that question: *How can a business be turned around quickly?*

A quick review of *In the BLACK—Nine Principles to Make Your Business Profitable* is appropriate here to set the stage for subsequent chapters. Here is a quick summary of the nine principles from that book:

The first three principles are for marketing; the second three for production; the last three for accounting—the three major functions of any small business.

1. Nothing happens until you make a sale!
2. A deal is only good when it is good for both parties.
3. Grow your business geometrically.

4. Pour on the communication.
5. Improve your internal processes.
6. Take what you have and make it better

7. Cash flow! Cash flow! Cash flow!
8. Know your business.
9. Plan for tomorrow.

There is another way of looking at the nine principles. Three are short-term in nature, three are medium-term, and three are long-term. Short-term principles are those that need to be addressed to-day. They have an immediate effect on company results.

SHORT-TERM PRINCIPLES:
1. Nothing happens until you make a sale!
4. Pour on the communication.
7. Cash flow! Cash flow! Cash flow!

Medium-term principles are those that need to be addressed but won't have an instant effect on the business like short-term principles. They are very important, however, and need to be addressed.

MEDIUM-TERM PRINCIPLES:
2. A deal is only good when it is good for both parties.
5. Improve your internal processes.
8. Know your business.

Long-term principles focus on critical issues that need to be addressed in any company over an extended period. But they will not change the results of the business overnight.

LONG-TERM PRINCIPLES:
3. Grow your business geometrically.
6. Take what you have and make it better.
9. Plan for tomorrow.

In the Black contains great material for small business owners looking to take a systems approach to their business processes to ensure profitability. *Red to Black in 30 Days,* however, is much more of a how-to book, helping you to answer the very valuable question: how do you turn troubled small businesses around quickly so they are profitable?

YOUR OBJECTIVE FOR READING THE BOOK

Now you know why I wrote the book. Here are a few ideas why you should read the book:

- It will develop your skills in helping troubled small businesses become profitable.
- It will help you become more proficient in these skills if you already have worked with troubled small businesses.
- It will help you master the models and processes necessary to make you a *Profit Expert.*

Many skills are involved in becoming proficient in turnaround strategies and tactics, and they are all outlined in this book. Included are project management skills with practical guidelines to help you set up projects correctly. *Red to Black in 30 Days* discusses the work that needs to be accomplished and how to complete it. It also covers setting up a timeframe in which you will complete that work and how you will be compensated for it.

The working relationship between the accountant and business owner needs to be thought through carefully so that each understands his roles and responsibilities. Accounting information and additional business management expertise are both valuable when advising a business owner through a turnaround situation. You will become a Profit Expert.

As a Profit Expert, you gain the business owner's respect with a focused analysis of the problems facing the business and your sound recommendations and workable solutions for resolving them. Your expertise will be valued *from the start*—a factor that will make you successful and secure your new position as Profit Expert. Your reputation as a turnaround specialist will spread and you will find new clients. Your reputation will help business clients find you.

You have an additional goal. You want to procure a one-year management and accounting agreement with the business owner as part of the turnaround process. This demonstrates that you know what you are doing and believe in the business as well as your process for saving it—it can survive this 30-day crisis and be a viable, healthy business one year from now and beyond.

You want to be associated with healthy, profitable, and growing companies. Your accounting and business management expertise can change your relationship with the business owner—all for the better.

BOOK ORGANIZATION

The book has nine chapters divided into three parts.

The **DISCOVER** phase includes Chapters One and Two. Chapter One focuses on becoming a Profit Expert. Chapter Two focuses on setting up the turnaround project correctly.

The **DEVELOP** phase covers the six action steps in the turnaround process with one chapter devoted to each step.

Chapter Three outlines Step 1: Assessing the Situation. Chapter Four describes Step 2 where you develop a succinct, practical turnaround plan based on the assessment results. You and the business owner should agree to use this plan as a guide during the turnaround project.

Chapters Five, Six, and Seven focus on action steps: controlling cash, reducing expenses and increasing revenue. You need to have control of certain systems—accounting, cash management, expense authorization—during the turnaround process. This planning document will assign roles and responsibilities.

Chapter Eight focuses on monitoring and reassessing the business situation after the 30-day turnaround period. In some cases, these steps will be enough to stabilize the business, which is our number one goal. In other cases, these 30 days represent the first iteration in the stabilization and growth process.

The **DOCUMENT** phase is described in Chapter Nine.

Chapter Nine allows you to document the major points that you and the business owner learned about his particular business. You have both assessed improvements made in the business during the 30 days and what still needs to be accomplished. Your task here is to document the business management expertise gained by both you and the business owner as you have worked diligently to make the business more successful.

Chapter Nine also allows you to document what you learned in enhancing your *Profit Expert* skills. These learning points should be written down and documented so that you do not have to relearn those skills.

Knowledge becomes business wisdom! Wisdom increases your expertise as an accountant, business manager, relationship builder and most importantly, Profit Expert. Wisdom includes what you have learned that will help you in your next turnaround project. Don't skip this step.

Frequently Asked Questions

Who should read this book?

Accountants and small business advisors, whether they are external or internal, who work with small businesses and want to be more effective must read this book. The concepts in *Red to Black in 30 Days* will make you a better advisor, *a Profit Expert*—to the small business owner.

A small business, for the purpose of this book, is any privately-held business with 20 employees or less. Decisions are made quickly, possibly by one person, without input from outsiders. One week in small businesses or even one day might see drastic changes in cash, prices, processes, procedures and people.

WHAT IS THIS 30 DAYS ALL ABOUT?
(The time it takes to go from Red to Black)

In this book, the thirty days is broken into 6 five-day work weeks. The timing—it could take 30 weeks or 30 hours—is not as important as the concepts and steps.

Of course some turnaround projects may take longer than six weeks. This book will outline a process that needs to be followed in turning small business problems around, irrespective of the time needed for the project. The emphasis, however, in this book will be on what can be accomplished in 30 days.

WHAT ARE REALISTIC EXPECTATIONS FOR 30 DAYS?

To show a profit! To do this, the small business must be able to adjust quickly to proposed changes. The process is important and sometimes 30 days is not long enough.

Because these businesses have less than 20 employees, they easily make quick adjustments—some within days and maybe hours to help implement turnaround strategies. This is a critical concept.

HOW SHOULD YOU READ THIS BOOK?

Sequentially at first, then as a reference manual. It is a process-driven book that will assist in turning an accountant into a turnaround expert. Important process models are provided to follow in assisting small businesses turn around.

The book provides a logical progression from assessment through execution of plans to stabilize small businesses that are in distress. It will follow the turnaround process and progress through three case studies. These cases are introduced at the end of this chapter.

Red to Black in 30 Days stays above the detail that some accountants love to see and analyze. That is intentional. In the following chapters, I address strategy, tactics and tools and how they are used but will not get lost in detail.

I realize that many small business accountants and many small business owners are female. But for the sake of clarity and succinctness, this book will be using masculine pronouns and adjectives. Please take no offense.

SUMMARY—WHERE YOU SHOULD BE AT THIS POINT

Many books have been written for the small business owner. This book focuses on small business accountants. The models, systems and processes outlined in this book will help you consult any small business but particularly those that are struggling.

You need to decide right now if this is the type of work you want to do in your accounting practice. You can make a difference in these troubled small businesses. Your skills as a Profit Expert and business manager are critical now!

As a business manager and advisor, you can outline a process to follow for stabilization of the business and help the small business owner make decisions that will lead to increased profitability. Effective communication of that information and your recommendations are critical in establishing and enhancing the relationship with the business owner.

INTRODUCTION
Key Learning Points

- You can make a difference for unprofitable small businesses. You can become a turnaround expert by using the strategies, tactics, tools and models presented in this book. *Red to Black in 30 Days* is your coach and guide through the process.

- Your differing roles as accountant, business manager, and Profit Expert are critical in small business turnaround situations. You will be a Profit Expert, providing advice that can help the small business owner make better, more effective decisions. You will make more money in your accounting practice with a variety of compensation methods.

- *In the BLACK* concepts form the foundation for the turnaround concepts in this book.

- Turnarounds can occur in 30 days or less in many cases—and you are the catalyst for those changes. This is especially true in organizations where there are less than 20 employees.

Not all small businesses will turnaround in 30 days. Some have inherent problems that might not be solved quickly. But if the small business is to be turned around, the concepts in this book will give invaluable help. *Red to Black in 30 Days* will focus on what will be done in 30 days.

CASE STUDY INTRODUCTION

Subsequent chapters will follow three small businesses as they attempt to quickly turn around from unprofitable and other adverse situations. Each small business has unique problems but a Profit Expert will help in all cases.

Here is the background information on each:

CASE I
Miriam's Art and Frame Shop

Miriam's Art and Frame Shop has been in business since 1995. It provides wholesale framing to designers and has 5 employees. As a sole proprietor, her financial statements reveal a healthy profit. But, she never seems to have any cash in the bank. Miriam hasn't taken a paycheck for three months.

You are Miriam's accountant and sister-in-law. You are quite competent but she doesn't use your services for more than quarterly financial statements and tax work. It is difficult to schedule Miriam's time to discuss business problems because she is always busy. You don't press the issue too much because it is hard to talk to a relative about financial problems.

You do know, however, there are serious cash problems in the business. And you will need to encourage a meeting with Miriam in the near future to make her aware of what the accounting information says about her business. You have some recommendations for Miriam if she will meet with you.

You are willing to become more involved in the business to ensure its success because you think the business has real potential. Miriam doesn't have much cash to pay you right now but you could agree to a small monthly fee and a percentage of future profits. She may agree to your help because she definitely needs it.

CASE II
Knecht Roofing and Construction

Knecht Roofing does roofing for several general contractors and any interested private parties. He has been in business since 2000. Kevin *seems* successful and is always busy. He brags about getting almost every bid he submits.

He should be rich. He has plenty of backlog but shows very low profit on his income statements. His wife does the bookkeeping for him but she needs help putting together monthly and quarterly financial statements.

Customers are happy with his work and he has great references. He needs two more roofers but doesn't know where the money will come from to pay them.

You are the outside accountant who generates quarterly tax and financial statements for Knecht. You will get the first call when Kevin realizes something is terribly wrong and his wife doesn't know the answers.

How will you get paid for your services? You don't want to be a partial owner of the company because working with Kevin on a constant basis would be difficult. Cash or a percentage of the profits or revenue might be the only way to go in this situation.

But you do need a new roof yourself. Maybe that is the way to get compensated.

CASE III

Sherwood's SureSave Market and Auto Repair

Sherwood's SureSave Market and Auto Repair has been on the same corner for over 25 years. Until recently, it had *cornered* the market for the area as the only convenience store, gas station and auto repair shop for almost a mile.

Tom, the owner, and his son, perform all the maintenance in the three auto bays located behind the store which remain busy all the time. They have three employees who work the convenience store and the front-end business. The gasoline pumps are old as is all of the front-end equipment.

Last year, a supermarket with discounted gas pumps opened on the opposite corner. Sales in the convenience store and at the pumps have declined ever since the new store opened. Profits have dropped significantly and before long, the business itself might fail!

You are the outside accountant that Tom calls when needing business advice. You know the business is currently experiencing many problems with more on the way. You have considered providing direction to Tom and his son.

They can afford your going accounting rate on a monthly basis. This may stretch your skills, however, because they need more help in marketing than they do with internal operations.

ONE

Being a Profit Expert

This chapter focuses on the big picture of being a Profit Expert and how, in that new role, you can assist small businesses in trouble. Every important model and process necessary in becoming a Profit Expert yourself is introduced in this chapter. You will become an expert by studying the subsequent chapters and through your own experience working through turnaround situations.

WHAT IS A PROFIT EXPERT?

In my mind, there are three degrees of accounting service—the bookkeeper, the accountant and the Profit Expert. The bookkeeper records transactions into the computer with direction and relatively little knowledge of how it impacts the big picture. In most situations, the bookkeeper will seek competent advice from an accountant.

The accountant has a working knowledge of how the financial statements are created and what they mean. An experienced accountant can also interpret financial statements and trends but generally stops short of giving meaningful management advice to business owners.

A Profit Expert is a financial advisor who has the skills of an accountant and also creates, enhances and turns around promising small businesses by providing direction in:

- Controlling cash effectively
- Reducing and minimizing expenses (including tax expenses)
- Increasing revenue

If you are not at the expertise level required to be a Profit Expert, you certainly will be at the end of this book. *Red to Black in 30 Days* provides the resources needed to help any small business with problems—even turnaround problems.

As mentioned before, often times small business owners have difficulty recognizing their own problems, let alone admitting them. Yet, there is never a shortage of problems. In general, small business owners wait too long to admit they have problems; then even longer to take action.

In some cases, the accountant may know critical information before the business owner. Thus, your role as an accountant and Profit Expert are paramount in all stages of turning the business around.

The fact is that numbers tell stories. The financial information an accountant provides may not be the first indicator of upcoming difficulty, but is instrumental in discovering the solution to the problems causing the difficulty.

YOUR OWN ACCOUNTING PRACTICE

Right now, a look at your own accounting practice is important to ensure this turnaround work is right for you. Questions come up in my consultations with accountants who work in turnaround situations that need to be addressed by you personally.

The first group of questions deal with **personal business issues** of growing your accounting practice. The second group of questions deal with the **technical business issues** of being a Profit Expert. And the third group of questions deal with your **relationship skills.** A Profit Expert needs to work with and communicate effectively with clients, particularly with clients in trouble.

PERSONAL BUSINESS ISSUES

These questions deal with your personal accounting practice. Perhaps you are currently grappling with these questions. They deal with the concept of working *on* your business, not *in* your business. These questions must be answered before you even approach an owner of a troubled business. The assumption made in the book is that you want to grow your business and this is one way to do it.

Is this work right for you?

You need to decide if this type work is right for you. Would you feel comfortable doing this type of work? You don't want to be in the middle of a project or six months down the road and then decide that you don't enjoy it.

This is the moment to spend some time working on the business not just *in* the business. When you work *in* your business, you are doing the everyday detail of getting the work completed. You could be working with business owners, other clients and potential clients. You are involved in the day-to-day operations of getting work done and rarely get a chance to look at the big picture of the business.

When you are working *on* your business, you step back from the day-to-day routine and look at the strategy of making the business more successful. What do you want to accomplish with the business per-se? Where do you want the business to be in a year or three years? If turnaround work will help you meet your business goals, then the work may be right for you.

Working with turnaround situations can be risky. Not all turnaround projects are successful. Maybe you won't get paid—at all. But the rewards can be high if you are successful. Not to mention these projects will build your expertise and reputation.

TECHNICAL BUSINESS ISSUES

Technical business issues deal with processes, reports, numbers and information needed to do your job as a Profit Expert. These are issues that must be addressed with the client in a turnaround situation. The focus here is usually on numbers that are in the accounting system of the business—if it is up to date. You need to be technically proficient to handle turnaround situations.

Symptoms that indicate a small business is in trouble

Symptoms are indications of underlying problems. The business owner might not even know that a problem exists. Perhaps he sees the symptom or even recognizes the problem but does not know how to react. You, as his accountant, can ensure he is aware of the problem and offer recommendations for improvement.

Symptoms must be treated in the short-term but more importantly, problems must be solved with long-term considerations. For instance, a loan may solve immediate cash flow needs, but given time, if the underlying cause doesn't change, cash will be in short supply again.

Symptoms of bigger problems commonly seen in troubled small businesses include the following (this list is certainly not all inclusive):

- Cash is in short supply. The bank account may not have enough money to pay the next payroll or current accounts payable.
- Collections of accounts receivable are slow to non-existent. Although people owe the business money, some for a long time, timely payments are slowing. This could reflect economic environment changes. Maybe it reflects no change from historical data but seems more critical now as cash becomes scarce.

- Sales are stagnant or slowing down. Management has become complacent with current sales levels, or worse, products are not going out the door as quickly as they once did. Orders are slowing down. Backlog is dwindling.

- Turnover is high. People are leaving constantly. Perhaps, they haven't been paid. Employees usually don't like instability in their employment and will change to more stable circumstances when ever possible.

- Customer complaints are increasing. The products and services are not performing the way they once did or perhaps customers' expectations have changed and the bar has been raised.

- Customers are moving toward competitors even though the perception is that the business' products and services are better. Maybe the products and services are not keeping up with competitors.

- The owner is working too much. There are too many fires to put out; some problems return constantly, and the owner never gets any time away from the business. This may not be new but the stress level is increasing and the problem has become more compelling.

These symptoms are often expressed openly in statements from business owners—they think about them constantly. Each of the following quotes could align with one or more of the symptoms mentioned above:

- "I work hard, yet I don't make a profit. Others seem to do it. Why can't I?"

- "According to the books I'm profitable, but the bank account doesn't show it. Why?"

- "Cash is always coming in but it goes out even faster. How can I better control my expenses?"

- "Is my business progress positive or negative?"

- "Is my business strong enough to weather bad times—even one month with no cash coming in?"

- "How do business professionals grade my company—my banker, for instance?"

- "Why do my most important employees leave the company?"

The accounting system, if it is up to date, has much information that can be used for analysis to make turnaround recommendations. If the accounting information is not up to date, then getting it up to date may be the first step—it is that important.

PROFIT EXPERT'S TOOL BOX

A Profit Expert needs technical tools and skills to be successful. The models and the resources identified in this chapter and explained more fully in subsequent chapters are essential to have in your Profit Expert's tool box. The models will help you gain competence and expertise. Experience will help you use these tools more effectively.

Three critical process models are presented in this book. These models, when implemented properly, will increase the probability that the turnaround project is successful.

THE UNIVERSAL PROJECT MANAGEMENT MODEL

The **Universal Project Management Model** is the predominant model in this book. In fact, everything in the book will somehow relate to this model. As you examine the Table of Contents, you will see that the book follows the Universal Project Management Model.

UNIVERSAL PROJECT MANAGEMENT MODEL

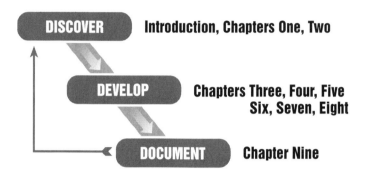

This **Universal Project Management Model** illustrates the conceptual steps that must be followed to organize, complete the work and evaluate and document the outputs. It helps in managing the work and the relationship with your client.

Perhaps more importantly, this model illustrates how to implement a continual improvement process. Continual improvement is mastering processes more efficiently better every day—to **DISCOVER, DEVELOP, and DOCUMENT** concepts and processes that work in the business and constantly improve them.

The focus is on effectiveness, doing the right things, and efficiency, doing things right. It is a business model that is followed when things are going well or when there are problems. This also allows you to develop your own business consulting and project management expertise.

When working with turnarounds, time is crucial and you only want to learn business lessons one time. You document these lessons in order to add them to that valuable body of business knowledge and wisdom. It is too expensive to learn the same business lessons over and over again.

The continuous improvement model followed in this book will also be followed in the business turnaround process. It works and will enhance your learning process faster.

UNIVERSAL TURNAROUND MODEL

The second important model outlined in this book is the **Universal Turnaround Model.** It is a subset of the Universal Project Management Model. This second model illustrates the process that can be followed during the actual turnaround work. It fits completely within the **DEVELOP** phase of the **Universal Project Management Model.**

This model illustrates the six major steps that should be followed in quick turnarounds. This model allows you to make process recommendations with little actual experience.

UNIVERSAL TURNAROUND MODEL

The six steps are as follows:

1. Assessing the situation—Chapter Three

2. Planning the turnaround project—Chapter Four

3. Improving cash management—Chapter Five

4. Reducing expenses—Chapter Six

5. Increasing revenue—Chapter Seven

6. Monitoring and reassessing the situation—Chapter Eight

The six steps correspond to the 30 day turnaround timeframe. Thirty days represents six 5-day work weeks. Many turnaround projects will take longer than six weeks, depending on the size of the business and its specific problems. Some businesses may turn around in 30 hours. And some businesses may never turn around.

Remember, the focus is on businesses with 20 or fewer employees, those that make changes quickly—maybe not effortlessly, but quickly. Most often, the smaller the business, the more agile and responsive it can be. It's like the analogy of a small boat to an oil tanker—the small boat can turn on a dime whereas the large ship requires much more time and attention to change its course.

Because the turnaround process is based on this model, the separate steps are discussed further in each chapter. In fact, each step has its own chapter.

The steps cannot be completed without the resources that are outlined in the center of the model:

- **Accounting Information**
- **Industry Data**
- **Advisory Group**

These resources are critical to the success of the turnaround project. Information from each of the resources should always be available and used in each of the different phases. That is why they are located in the center of the model. These resources are described more fully in Chapter Two.

UNIVERSAL SCORE CARD MODEL

The third model is the **Universal Score Card Model (Example)** which is illustrated on the next page. This model is also a subset of the **Universal Project Management Model.** This model illustrates a typical Score Card for a small business. The purpose of the Score Card is to regularly monitor the progress made in different areas of the company.

To a business, the Universal Score Card is much like what a dashboard is to a driver of a vehicle. A quick glance at the dashboard gives the driver needed information which is immediately used in adjusting the course and speed of the vehicle. The Score Card can do the same for a business owner. A quick glance at the Score Card will let the owner know what adjustments must be made to better manage the course and speed of his business.

The Universal Score Card is designed during the **DISCOVER** phase of the project and used in the **DEVELOP** phase during all six steps of the turnaround model. You will see Score Cards designed and used in the three cases at the end of each chapter as well. Universal Score Cards are also used in the **DOCUMENT** phase to capture major learning points from the turnaround project.

UNIVERSAL SCORE CARD MODEL (EXAMPLE)

Description	Week 1 Assessment	Week 2 Planning	Week 3 Cash	Week 4 Expenses	Week 5 Revenue	Week 6 Reassess	Target
Cash in the bank							
Accounts Receivable over 30/90 days old							
Bills (cash out) owed in the next week							
End of Month Accounting ratios							
Weekly Sales							
Monthly Sales							
Cash sales vs. Credit							
Number of jobs							
Revenue per job							

Score Cards are customized for the specific small business for which you are working and place the focus on the key business indicators that need improvement during the turnaround process.

The Score Card provides a quick and easy look at the status of the business. The extreme right-hand column indicates what the target number is for that particular category. That makes it easier to ascertain progress as you move toward the target. The Score Card can be monitored on a daily basis but most definitely on a weekly basis.

The Universal Score Card reflects progress in the three areas in which a Profit Expert works:

- **Controlling cash**
- **Reducing and minimizing expenses**
- **Increasing revenue**

Just as an athletic coach encourages players with numbers or statistics, so you can coach a small business owner from the numbers on your Score Card. The Score Card concept is discussed in Chapter Four on planning. Another good resource on Score Cards is my first book *In the Black—Nine Principles to make your business profitable.*

The three models illustrated above comprise the foundation of what is needed in your Profit Expert's tool box. They are technical in nature and are a great resource in your turnaround work.

RELATIONSHIP SKILLS

Relationship skills is the third area considered before entering into small business turnaround situations. You may be very astute technically but weak in communication skills. "Soft skills" are as important as the technical skills in successfully completing the turnaround project.

Are you and the small business owner able to work together throughout a difficult turnaround project?

If you can't get along with the business owner, the turnaround project will be miserable. This is the time to talk about the relationship with the business owner of the troubled business. What type of relationship is necessary if you are to work together closely on this turnaround project?

Will the small business owner listen to you?

Over the years I have learned that the message is not as important as the way the message is presented. The key is to speak as one having authority.

In other words, a person who answers boldly and with a smile will always have more respect than the timid, sour-faced accountant—even though the latter may be more experienced.

Ask bold questions. The fact is you have more accounting knowledge than the business owner. And, it's likely that the business owner will ask you a question that will require consideration or research. That's all right—don't be afraid to say, "Let me get back to you on that." But say it boldly, enthusiastically, and with a smile.

One critical element of being a trusted advisor is not necessarily having the right answers but *having the right questions.*

Here are some bold and critical questions for the business owner. Bold questions build relationships. These questions are part of the business assessment which is described in Chapter Three. However, if you cannot get through these questions, there is no relationship:

What is working well in your business right now?

What is not working so well?

What is your business model? Or phrased differently, how does the business make money?

How is the business model working?

What do your customers want from you?

Can you deliver what is needed in a cost-effective manner?

Who is your competition and what are they doing?

There should be a mutual commitment to get the business turned around. The small business owner should be as committed as you are. These questions will let you know how committed the business owner is.

QUALIFICATIONS

The accountant can be more knowledgeable about the business profits than anyone else within the business—often more so than the owner. The accountant is intimately familiar with the financial processes, transactions, and structure that make up the profit and loss in the business. A qualified small business accountant is the most qualified advisor a business owner has when seeking to maximize business profitability.

As an accountant, you may have valuable information that the business owner needs to know but is not currently using to make important business decisions or to help run the business more profitably.

As a Profit Expert, you will become more proactive than you have been with the client—maybe weekly or even daily instead of monthly, or quarterly, or annually. This is especially true in a turnaround situation.

Business advising puts another light on the importance of accountants and the information provided for the small business. Many times financial reports such as income statements and balance sheets, are prepared and delivered to the business owner without any discussion. This is an opportunity lost. You can easily position yourself in an advisory role by offering to interpret and translate the financial statements.

Turnaround steps put the work process into a more objective format so that better recommendations can be made. Chapter Two focuses specifically on how to set up a project agreement with the business owner. In doing so, it is important to ensure that both your needs and the business owner's needs are met.

Additionally, an important qualification is to be a Professional Bookkeeper or Certified Public Accountant so that you understand small business accounting issues, and can work with a variety of businesses confidently. Furthermore, your cards bearing the "PB" or "CPA" designation provide essential credibility.

You must have business cards and letterhead that carry a message alerting businesses of your turnaround skills. Identify yourself as a *Profit Expert.*

Always look forward to opportunities to learn and develop new skills. Subscribe to trade journals and become involved in organizations that will hone your skills.

Your best tool, of course, is the ability to analyze the accounting information thoroughly and compare your findings to published industry data. This comparison will yield critical information indicating where changes must be made in order for a business to compare favorably with others in the industry.

There are a number of analytical tools available today that weren't available ten years ago. These software programs can make even the least experienced accountant look like a seasoned Profit Expert. Business assessment software programs, when loaded with a company's financial information, deliver professional and thorough business advice.

Frequently Asked Questions

Why should you care about all this?

The most obvious answer is because it can bring you greater respect from others in the marketplace, increased confidence in yourself, and more money. The less self-serving answer is because businesses need you.

Most new businesses fail in the first year. Often this is because they didn't know what they were doing with their money. In many cases they surrendered their home, their savings, and self-worth when their dream businesses closed. *Red to Black in 30 Days* will give you the expertise to know how your accounting practice can help these types of business owners.

How do you react when a business owner approaches you?

Enthusiastically! You should be eager for the opportunity to assist the business in becoming what it should be and to help the owner earn what he is worth. Certainly, this does not include any guarantees, but it should include some real encouragement.

Relieve the embarrassment with reassurance that business problems are not uncommon. Focus on how his strengths will complement your strengths.

How much hope should you give a business owner?

A lot! In a turnaround situation, *hope* is the major product that you sell. Things will be better in the future. Usually, every business deserves your rigorous attention for at least one month to see if the business can be viable when profitable changes are implemented.

This is not about products or markets; it's about internal management.

How do you keep from getting emotionally involved?

Short of losing sleep, the more emotionally involved you are, the more effective you will be in working with the owner. The more passion you show for the success of the business, the more the owner will know that you are the right person to be his advisor.

The counterpoint to that is that you still need to be the objective voice in the relationship. That is why the business owner hired you.

However, if you notice that the turnaround project is impacting your health, pull back. Bring in other advisors to help solve the problem.

How do you react when the business owner ignores problems and recommendations?

There is not much you can do if the owner has little resolve to improve the business situation. Remember, it is his business and he can choose to react apathetically.

However, if the business owner unknowingly ignores problems, you need to speak to him like a friend. Let him know that you recognize it is his decision, but if it were you, these would be some concerns that you would have. Show trends and the direction they are heading. Describe likely scenarios given the business's current financial position. Give time frames that will demonstrate how much time is left. You don't wish to be an alarmist; you want to give a friendly warning.

What if you dislike the business owner?

Relationships are very important. But the issue here is not whether or not you like the business owner. The real question is can you work closely over at least a month's time? You don't have to like him if you can tolerate him for a while. The relationship might change over time. The bigger question is: Can you work with him for a year? Beyond the turnaround process you want to have a management contract for at least that long.

Certainly, if the business owner is engaged in illegal or unethical practices, then that is a stronger indicator for not working with the owner than dislike.

How can you help if you don't have much experience in the industry? Do you need to have done this before?

Certainly experience helps. But, just like everything else in life, you have to do something for the first time. This book will lead you step by step through the process so you will appear as an expert, even though you may not feel like one at the start. Thus, the critical piece is the *process,* not the *industry.*

What if the business has no cash? Can you still help?

Maybe. This is definitely a relationship issue. If the business is in an industry that has a bright or stable future, and the business owner is willing to follow your advice, the two of you can get the business back on track. But the most common indicator of success is the owner's attitude.

Obviously, the next question is, "But how do I get paid?" Check out Chapter Two for answers to this question.

What other resources are available to help become more proficient at being a Profit Expert?

Universal Accounting Center offers a workshop for small business accountants to help them realize their potential as *Profit Experts.*

SUMMARY—WHERE YOU SHOULD BE AT THIS POINT

You have decided that turnaround work is right for you and your accounting practice. Turnaround projects can help you build your accounting practice.

Now the question is about the necessary skills and tools to do the work. The rest of the book will provide the guidance—tools, models and processes—necessary to become an expert in quick small business turnarounds.

CHAPTER ONE
BEING A PROFIT EXPERT
Key Learning Points

- Experts surround businesses on every side—media experts, legal experts, computer experts, even marketing experts. Each specializes in one or more particular areas of business. A profit and growth expert is someone who can look beyond the obvious in business and provide analysis and direction that will aid the business owner in improving business profits and growth.

- The term *Profit Expert* describes an accountant who has expertise in advising small businesses in controlling cash, reducing expenses and increasing revenue.

- Profit Experts have the technical tools, models, processes and the relationship skills to lead turnaround projects to successful outcomes. They can effectively spot symptoms of problems and assess problem situations.

- The **Universal Project Management Model** provides the foundation (**DISCOVER—DEVELOP—DOCUMENT**) for all turnaround work outlined in the book, from creating an initial agreement with the business owner to evaluating the completed project. This model illustrates how continual improvement in each turnaround step leads to better and better results.

- The **Universal Turnaround Model** outlines the six steps in the turnaround process and the resources necessary to make the work successful. It is a subset of the **Universal Project Management Model** and all aspects of the model are important in providing you with direction.

- **The Universal Score Card** is a way to monitor progress during the **DEVELOP** phase. Profit Experts use Score Cards to teach business principles and coach business owners in strong management skills.

- Accounting information is the most important resource you have for analyzing the business, making recommendations about how to turn the business around and helping the business grow. This information, along with the models and other resources provided in this book will move you quickly along the learning curve in becoming a Profit Expert and turnaround guru.

- All chapters of this book provide resources to help any small business accountant become a Profit Expert and enhance skills as a turnaround expert. The tools and the models in this book are your coach.

CASE I

Miriam's Art and Frame Shop

Being Miriam's accountant doesn't mean that much actually. You fill out the quarterly payroll reports and that's about it. You don't know much about the day-to-day operations at all given her in-house office manager takes care of the daily bookkeeping. You wish you were more involved.

She told you that there is not enough money in the bank to pay the employee taxes for the quarter. Something is wrong in the business but you don't know what. You would like to talk with her more about the problem. You don't want her to get on the wrong side of the Internal Revenue Service.

How would you approach Miriam about the possibility of helping her with this problem? Will Miriam's being a family member help or hinder your communication with her? What information would you like to know about Miriam's business before you see more detailed information in the financial statements?

This could lead to your becoming much more involved in her business than you already are or may want. Having no cash in the bank could be a real problem in being paid for your work. Right now you don't charge her much more than just expenses to do quarterly reports. But there are other modes of compensation, such as partial ownership of the art and frame shop if the turnaround is successful.

On the other hand, this might give you a great opportunity to expand your accounting and business consulting expertise. You already have ideas about what can be accomplished in Miriam's business to improve performance.

After all you are a *Profit Expert!*

CASE II

Knecht Roofing and Construction

You are the accountant for Knecht Roofing and Construction. You do work on Kevin Knecht's quarterly payroll taxes and create the quarterly financial statements. But he usually does his yearly income taxes himself and might be hiding something from you or deducting more expenses on his taxes than you would consider appropriate. He seems to share less and less information with you about his actual financial dealings.

At any rate, he recently asked to meet with you for help with his quarterly payroll taxes. Although you haven't spent much time examining his overall financial statements, you had noticed some numbers that look out of sync.

Now is a chance for you to use your accounting expertise and perhaps help him through some rough times in his business. However, you would need to be more involved than you are presently.

What would you do in your next meeting with Kevin that would help him realize that you could be a valuable resource to him?

The issues, at first glance, seem to focus on sales and profit. Profit does not seem to correlate well with sales. This seems somewhat odd because Kevin has enough business. Something is happening in the expense line that needs some attention. Expenses are too high or maybe the sales just can't support the amount of expenses that the business is carrying.

Help is definitely needed. And you can help because you are a *Profit Expert!*

CASE III

Sherwood's SureSave Market and Auto Repair

You are the accountant for Sherwood's SureSave Market and Auto Repair (an independent convenience store and auto repair shop).

Sales have been declining since that X?)@! grocery store opened across the street. Profits are waning, and before long the store could be losing money. Gasoline sales are steadily declining. The pumps are old and need to be replaced, and you are worried that gas is leaking from the tanks. Thank goodness the auto repair bays have kept busy.

You agree that trends are heading south and that something needs to happen quickly. At first glance the issues seem to be: business redirection in light of the major grocery store across the street and reestablishment of a profitable income stream.

Tom Sherwood, the father and owner is just now realizing the critical nature of addressing these issues immediately.

You can help when you take charge, because you are a *Profit Expert!*

TWO

Setting Up the Project

You have decided that turnaround work is for you. It can help your practice grow; you can secure better clients and make more money. You also know that your skills and expertise are already in place or that the coaching in this book can provide the guidance necessary. This chapter focuses on setting up the turnaround project correctly: what needs to be done by you, the accountant, before any other steps are taken.

When a small business is in trouble, it means that it is no longer "business as usual." Changes need to occur in order to restore the business's profitability. This also means that your accountant's point-of-view must widen as you look at the business as a whole. To use an old cliché, it is like changing your view of the trees to the overall forest.

That's okay. This book will provide you with the resources to effectively change your perspective. Keep reading. The models and case studies will bring you up-to-date. This chapter will prepare you as a Profit Expert to facilitate those changes. Your expertise will be used for much more than just filling out tax forms.

WHAT IS MEANT BY SETTING UP THE PROJECT?

For the purposes of this book, the term *project* implies a large undertaking, in this case, the specific 30-day task of stabilizing a small business and preparing it for growth. It means that you are establishing a framework in which you can work together with the business owner to get the business turned around. This framework defines the roles, responsibilities and work processes to be followed during the turnaround period and beyond if you are working under a year-long management contract.

As mentioned before, I frequently hear the following three questions from accountants:

- *What do I do with a small business in trouble?*
- *How do I get paid or compensated for my work?*
- *And how should I formalize this relationship with the business owner?*

The answer to each of these questions is found in setting up the project correctly.

Here is a quick answer for the first question *(What do I do with a small business in trouble?)*: Well, you can do a lot! What does that look like exactly? It means you know the process and have the resources, accounting and management tools, necessary in turning the business around. You cannot guarantee the business will turn around, but you can guarantee the process and the quality of your work.

The process is the most important resource you have. The models presented in this book provide the process methods if you don't know them already.

Here is a quick answer to question 2 *(How do I get compensated?)*: Obviously, you must be compensated for your work. This compensation is critical to the success of your own accounting practice and business. Maybe you need cash now to run or expand your accounting practice. Maybe you can't wait for the business to see profits to occur so you can take a percentage as compensation. If either of these situations is true, then taking on a turnaround project may not work for you at the present time.

Compensation might be in the form of an hourly, daily or monthly stipend. But if a company has no cash, then asking for cash payment may not work at all. You may consider more creative payment methods like a percentage of future profits, a percentage of ownership in the business or possibly a barter of some sort. Each form of compensation has its advantages and disadvantages.

As the cases develop at the end of each chapter, you will see different methods of compensation used in each situation. These methods are not all inclusive but do represent some good alternatives.

Here is a quick answer to question 3 *(How should a relationship with the business owner be formalized?):* Most assuredly, this relationship you have with the business owner will change—for the better or the worse. The relationship changes because the work changes. If you do nothing, your relationship with the business owner will change anyway—he could be out of business and you will be out a client.

This work will be different from previous tasks performed for the business owner. This job requires you to develop a new level of accounting information, interpret that information quickly yet accurately and make appropriate operational recommendations in order to promote quick, profitable changes in the business. It may not have been necessary for you to make these tough recommendations before. However, it is now.

It also means establishing processes and systems that sustain the turnaround. You will probably be the chief architect of these systems and accurate and timely accounting information is critical in sustaining new processes and systems.

PROJECT MANAGEMENT

Project management was introduced briefly in Chapter One, now will be discussed in more detail. Understanding and using proper project management skills are critical to your success as a Profit Expert. The turnaround project sets up the changing relationship with the business owner, how you work with him and what you will do.

Project management involves three phases—**DISCOVER**—**DEVELOP**—**DOCUMENT.** These phases follow the continual improvement model that has been mentioned before and will be referred to in subsequent chapters. The business owner may not be aware of these improvement phases, but you must be!

The three phases of the **Universal Project Management Model** are illustrated in the diagram below:

UNIVERSAL PROJECT MANAGEMENT MODEL

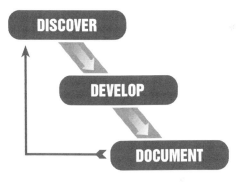

This model can be helpful to you as an accountant and has nothing to do with accounting. You need to become a trusted advisor and Profit Expert during the turnaround process and using this model ensures you are doing the right thing at the right time. The **Universal Project Management Model** will make that process much easier.

DISCOVER

There are two critical steps within the **DISCOVER** phase of the project: Designing the turnaround project and getting a written agreement.

DESIGN THE TURNAROUND PROJECT

This step includes the following:

1. Identify major problems (or at least the symptoms) in the small business that make it unprofitable and develop a level of assurance that you can be successful in turning the business around.

    Does the business owner even realize there is a problem? You may be the one who identifies the problem or maybe the owner comes to you after identifying the problem.

2. Communicate the problems that you see to the business owner and convince him that something must be done to save the business— and quickly.

    Most business owners seem overly optimistic about the future outcomes of the business. It seems like there is always a big sale "right around the corner" that will save the business. Unfortunately, those sales rarely materialize. For that reason, your initial offer to help the business often goes unheeded. Give it a week or two and the business owner will be ready to talk.

3. Determine what the desired results will be. What happens if you do nothing right now? What will the company look like when it is successful in improving cash, expenses and revenue?

4. Determine action steps (referred to as *scope of work*) to complete and reach the desired results.

5. Establish your role as an accountant, more specifically as a Profit Expert in the project, outlining roles for you and the business owner during the turnaround process. A written agreement is more about memory than trust.

Hopefully, a solid relationship with the business owner is set before problems occur. When the business owner discovers a problem, he comes to you. When you discover a problem or a troubling trend, you inform him.

In a turnaround situation, accounting information must be analyzed accurately and recommendations made. But, if the recommendations are not implemented as needed and in a timely manner, then the outcome may still result in business failure. Clear communication between you and the business owner is imperative.

Here are some guidelines to help communicate:

- Communicate problem symptoms—these symptoms could indicate deeper problems in the business.

- Stick to the facts as you describe the underlying problem or problems. Show numerical evidence from the accounting reports that back your position.

- Suggest the implications of not doing anything.

- Suggest that mistakes have been made but those mistakes are not uncommon. Other business owners have made the same mistakes.

- These situations and mistakes can be overcome and you are in the best position to make those changes. You can turn the business around and you can do it right now.

- Sell HOPE! Success and profit are attainable!

- Make sure the business owner knows he is better off because he has you as an advisor.

- Suggest an action plan, clearly stating solution steps or process of improvement.

- Introduce the need for a written project agreement.

The second step in the **DISCOVER** phase is:

GET A WRITTEN AGREEMENT

The agreement you have had in the past will not be sufficient for this new type of work. A letter of agreement will solidify the new understanding you have with the owner about this turnaround project. An oral agreement, in most cases, is not sufficient.

A written agreement protects everyone. This may be no more than a two-page document or it can be longer depending on how detailed you think it has to be for both parties to understand. But two pages are usually sufficient.

Decision-making should be addressed in the agreement as well as your compensation—how much and when it occurs.

The agreement should answer these questions:

What your client wants from you

The business owner wants to be successful in business. That means, first and foremost, the business is profitable. It also means that the business is expanding and that expenses are under control. The business owner probably wants to retain as many current employees as possible without having to let valuable, loyal employees go. In most cases, it is the processes that need to change, not the people.

What you want from your client

You definitely want to get paid. And you want to have access to him or her in order to gather and analyze necessary information. This project could take all your time in the next month. How will you be compensated? Usually, we accountants don't like working for our health alone. Here are some methods to consider:

- Cash payment based on some sort of rate schedule
- Percentage of future profits
- Barter future services
- Percentage of ownership in the business
- Some other type of compensation

The written agreement establishes roles for everyone involved in the turnaround project

Once it is decided that the turnaround project is necessary and time is critical, then it is important to understand exactly who is going to do what throughout the process.

Project work steps

What does success look like? And what is the accompanying timeframe? Although success and profitability may not be guaranteed, your payment may depend upon it.

And how should you handle changes in project work steps? In most cases, you must compile specific data or run assessments before recommendations and interventions can be made. You can usually perform this analysis in your role as Profit Expert.

Agreement outline

An outline for your written agreement might include:

- Identification of the problem
- Description of the working relationship
- Project work detail, including roles, responsibilities and decision making process
- Outputs from both you and the business owner
- Compensation—how much and when you will be paid
- Projected schedule for completion

Sometimes not all of these issues will be addressed in a written agreement. It depends on your needs and those issues that are unique to each turnaround situation. However, these questions or issues need to be addressed between you and the business owner before any significant work can be done.

Sample agreement letters are included with the case studies at the end of this chapter.

DEVELOP

The **DEVELOP** phase of the **Universal Project Management Model** entails doing the actual turnaround work. The **Universal Turnaround Model** illustrates what is involved in doing the work. There are six major steps involved with three major resources that can be used at any time to help complete the steps.

UNIVERSAL TURNAROUND MODEL

This **Universal Turnaround Model** begins with the Assessing step in the upper right and moves clockwise through Monitoring and Reassessing. Resources, outlined in the middle, can be used anytime throughout the process to move the project forward.

This model describes the work steps in the actual turnaround work. Each step will be discussed in much more detail in subsequent chapters. A chapter is devoted to each of the turnaround steps, beginning in Chapter Three: Assessing the Situation. This particular turnaround model is a guideline for the actual work and is iterative in nature. Once the steps are completed, you start over again within the continual improvement framework.

The six steps are as follows:

1. Assessing the situation—Chapter Three

2. Planning the turnaround project—Chapter Four

3. Improving cash management—Chapter Five

4. Reducing expenses—Chapter Six

5. Increasing revenue—Chapter Seven

6. Monitoring and reassessing the situation—Chapter Eight

Once this monitoring step is complete, the cycle can begin again if necessary.

As you can see, one chapter in the book focuses on each of these six steps.

The steps are not complete without the resources that are outlined in the center of the model:

- **Accounting Information**
- **Industry Data**
- **Advisory Group**

These resources are critical to the success of the turnaround project. Information from each resource should always be available and may be used in each of the different phases. That is why they are located in the center of the model; the steps are not complete without them.

ACCOUNTING INFORMATION

Each of the turnaround steps depends on accounting information to be successful. Some indicators or trends will be known by the accountant before anyone else. The bias in this book is toward the importance of accounting information.

Some problems can be devastating if not handled quickly. To begin with, a current Balance Sheet and Profit and Loss Statement will provide most of the information you need. But the more detailed information will be explained in the Assessment Chapter.

INDUSTRY DATA

There is a wealth of information on nearly every industry. This information can practically make you an overnight expert on virtually any business type. And it can generally be found online, in libraries, trade journals, and at Universal Accounting Center.

This allows you to compare your own business to accounting statistics from similar businesses within your industry. It identifies industry weaknesses and can indicate your company's strengths and weaknesses as compared with other companies in the same industry.

ADVISORY GROUP

An advisory group can provide outside expertise, objectivity and practical advice in the decision-making process. The group is usually comprised of the business owner, his accountant, an attorney, a banker and an insurance agent, depending on the business owner's needs and the group members' expertise.

An Advisory Group may not be appropriate in all cases. Much depends on who the business owner feels comfortable with and how much information he is willing to share with this group. Their only purpose is to give the business owner good advice on how to turn the business around and should not be motivated by any other agenda.

DOCUMENT

The **DOCUMENT** phase is also critical in the overall **Universal Project Management Model.** While the exciting work may be done in the DISCOVER and DEVELOP phases, the DOCUMENT phase is where you evaluate the work completed and capture the major learning points from the turnaround project and in your personal accounting practice.

MEASURING AND EVALUATING THE PROJECT

Measurement and evaluation of the project are necessary but tricky. You cannot guarantee turnaround success. Even with your best accounting and consulting efforts, the business might not succeed. Perhaps the problems are too far advanced to stabilize.

The best measurement tool you can use is the **Universal Score Card** that was introduced in Chapter One. If the targets were set up accurately (found in the far right-hand column), then the actual progress in the selected categories should approach the targets as the weeks go by.

The biggest measurement, obviously, can be found in the business's profitability. An increase in profits is the number one indicator of business success and probably your own compensation. For compensation purposes, profit should be determined on an accrual basis. It is easier to calculate and you can get a check every month—as long as the business is profitable.

Frequently Asked Questions

Do the steps in the Universal Turnaround Model correspond with the 30 days outlined in **Red to Black?**

Yes, basically. Many turnaround projects will take longer than six weeks, depending on the size of the business and its specific problems. Some businesses may turn around in 30 hours. And some businesses may never turn around. This book assumes that the 30 days is comprised of six 5-day work weeks. The six-step process will work irrespective of the time involved. However, the guideline used for this book is thirty days.

What about work guarantees?

You can guarantee your time and your passion and most importantly, the work you do. But you cannot guarantee profits. There are too many factors at play, particularly those for which the business owner is responsible.

What are the factors you can guarantee? Your work may include time spent on the project, the actual financial statements you prepare, business plan preparation, but not necessarily implementation. You don't control that; the owner does.

Proper management of Accounts Payable and Accounts Receivable and of the Cash account can also be guaranteed. As you will see in Case III, you cannot guarantee convenience store and gasoline sales success when a new, strong competitor moves in across the street.

Be careful what you agree to—guarantee your work but not the success of the turnaround project. Many factors play into the success of the turnaround project. Yours is only one. As the accountant, what are your work products or outputs? Ensure you can control what you are measured on. Outputs are work products that you can complete, and practically guarantee.

Keep in mind that your goal is to not only turn the business around but to garner at least a one-year management contract with the business. This indicates that you have faith in the business as a long-term entity.

You want the business to be profitable and you want to be compensated for your contributions. However, even if the business is not profitable, this does not mean you didn't perform the work you agreed to as the accountant. You should still be compensated as specified by the agreement between you and the business owner.

What are the possible risks for you as an accountant?

Becoming involved with a troubled business can be risky business unless you're careful. The risk is greatest if you accept partial ownership of the business as compensation. In this case use common sense by involving an attorney who can structure the agreement in such a way that you do not become owner *until* the business is successful. That way, if the existing owner fails to accept your advice and the company continues to decline, you're not at risk.

That is why I don't recommend taking a percentage of ownership as compensation. It is too complicated. I recommend taking a percentage of the profits or additional profits over the course of a year. This year includes the time required to complete the turnaround project and the remainder of that same year. This gives you a chance to enhance your relationship with the business owner.

If your agreement simply provides you a lump sum, hourly income, or a percentage of profits as a contractor, the risk is that you may not get a dime for your effort. If the business has a bad payment history, there is no reason to think that will change without effort.

What are major red flags in setting up a turnaround project?

The business owner is ultimately responsible for the success of the business. Recognizing that, the business owner is responsible for implementing your recommendations unless you have complete control of the business. If the owner isn't motivated, or doesn't respect your advice, the likelihood of a turnaround is remote.

Lack of integrity on the part of the owner is a large red flag; for example, if the owners are hiding income from the IRS or are dishonest with partners and key employees. An owner that has served jail time is a huge red flag because it generally indicates that this individual has a history and reputation of illegal and dishonest dealings.

What if you discover the business owner is doing something illegal?

A snake is still a snake regardless of what you call it. If the owner lacks integrity in the eyes of the law, what makes you believe he will be honest with you? If you discover this before the agreement, have a talk with the owner and let him know that this will not be tolerated. If he accepts your judgment and you feel he is sincere, then you are ready to move on. If he does not, wish him luck and leave him to his own demise.

If you're not sure, simply get a credit report on the potential client to see for yourself what his past experience has been. A low score not only indicates an owner with questionable integrity, but it also signifies that financing is out of the question.

What about the timing of the project?

This process of setting up the project with the owner and determining what will be done and by whom need not take long. In fact, it should only take a few days. The hard part is getting the business owner to realize that changes must be made in order for the business to survive—the sooner the better.

Each phase equates to one week. Thus, six steps equals six weeks or 30 days. Turnaround projects take time. So if you are involved, be prepared to work hard—and on weekends, if necessary.

SUMMARY—WHERE YOU SHOULD BE AT THIS POINT

The focus of this chapter is to outline the turnaround project on paper as much as possible before doing any of the actual work. You have thought through every contingency that could occur during your relationship or one-year management contract.

The two major steps in the **DISCOVER** phase are designing the turnaround project and getting a written agreement for your work with the business owner. You should have a picture of what the project looks like as well as a written agreement defining success and the roles and responsibilities you and the business owner are to assume for the next 30 days.

Not only do you want to be a business advisor for the turnaround project but also for a year after the project is completed. This turnaround business plan communicates to the owner your confidence that the business will stabilize during the next 30 days and then grow beyond that.

CHAPTER TWO
SETTING UP THE PROJECT
Key Learning Points

- The better you complete this step of the project, the better the project will run (and generally, the more quickly it will be completed).

- Communication skills are critical during this phase of the turnaround project, particularly as you, the accountant, describe business problems to the owner and suggest alternative outcomes based on your recommendations.

- Project management skills are critical. The **Universal Project Management Model (DISCOVER-DEVELOP-DOCUMENT)** provides a continual improvement framework in which all work can be completed.

- Accounting information is critically important to the successful completion of the turnaround. Its importance during this phase of the project must be established and emphasized.

- Compensation for your work in the turnaround project and ongoing management involvement needs to be agreed upon. A payment schedule would also be helpful.

- It is important to protect yourself with a written agreement. The written agreement should include roles and responsibilities for you and the business owner. The actual work steps should also be outlined in the written agreement. When completed, the written agreement should include:

  - Identification of the problem
  - Description of the working relationship

- Project work detail, including roles, responsibilities and the decision-making process
- Outputs from both you and the business owner
- Compensation—how much and when you will be paid
- Projected schedule for completion

• Measurement criteria of what the completed project looks like must be clear. You can guarantee your work but not the profitable outcome of the turnaround project.

• There are risks for you. As an accountant you cannot guarantee business success, but you can guarantee your own contributions to the project. Be careful what you agree to. The business owner himself is unable to guarantee much either.

CASE I
Miriam's Art and Frame Shop

So, you finally mustered the courage to speak with Miriam, your sister-in-law, about her business problems. You thought it would be a tough discussion, but she was easier to talk to than you anticipated. She knew there were problems that needed to be addressed immediately.

A quick look at the available cash in the bank confirmed to both of you that this is a huge problem. This problem threatens the viability and survival of the business. And the problem is immediate, as in *today!* Other problems exist, but controlling cash is by far the most pressing.

You committed to spend more time in the business and help Miriam through this turnaround process.

As she is strapped for cash, a request for payment would not only be pointless but somewhat offensive considering you're family. So, since you plan to be part of her family for the rest of your life, you requested a percentage of the profits.

She agreed to give you $1,000 a month fee or 25% of the profit, whichever is greater (providing you make it through the first 30 days) in exchange for your ongoing services—advice, counsel, accounting services, and general business acumen. You will work on a written agreement defining the work to be done and your professional relationship. This turnaround must take place in less than six months.

You will spend at least eight hours a week in the business, spread throughout the week. You cannot afford to spend more time than this because of your current compensation agreement. Most of that time will be onsite and some will be spent working in your own office, at least until the business is functioning smoothly and profitably.

Cash would not be affected by your involvement for at least six months. Then you can jointly decide how the cash will be divided between reinvestment, Miriam and you. After six weeks, you see the time commitment changing to about eight hours per month.

The benefits to Miriam are these:

- She will have someone taking responsibility for the administrative portion of the business.

- She is much better off if the turnaround project is successful. Yes, she surrenders a percentage of future profit to you, but currently she is experiencing no profit at all. Survival is at stake. She might give up 20-25% of future profits, but she could lose the whole business if she doesn't do anything. The risk is minimal for her.

The benefits to you, the accountant and Profit Expert, include:

- The perceived time investment with Miriam's business is minimal— at least for what you are currently envisioning, and you don't need a lot of cash now.

- You can become more involved in the day-to-day business decisions. More overall business involvement will further develop your skills and your accounting knowledge. You feel that you have enough time to generate revenue from other projects.

Your risks include an unsuccessful turnaround and greater time requirements than anticipated.

Already you have an idea regarding what can be done in her business. You're also aware of the key indicator of success—total sales and profit. Further analysis is required.

Here is your letter of agreement with Miriam:

Dear Miriam,

It was a pleasure to meet with you yesterday to discuss the current condition of your business. I sincerely feel that, together, we can make this business the type of company you envisioned when you created it.

Below is a brief description of our agreement:

Project Work

During the next 30 days, I will focus on cash improvement strategies that can provide a more satisfactory bank account balance. I will begin by assessing the position of your company and analyzing current business practices. I will then make recommendations for change. Then jointly, we will arrive at a plan that is comfortable for you that will accomplish your objectives.

Outputs

With your current cash flow needs, you will work to establish a balance in the bank account that is maintainable, and will provide for your ongoing needs, as well as emergencies that may come along. These techniques may require changes in your current business procedures, but in the long run will assure greater control over one of your most important assets—Cash.

Compensation

I look forward to being a valuable part of your management team. During the next several weeks, I expect to devote at least 8 hours per week to this project. Once our objectives have been met, I envision spending the time necessary to work as your profit and growth consultant. In return, we agreed that I will receive a $1,000 per month fee or 25% of the profit, whichever is greater, for the next twelve months. An accrual method of accounting will be used for determining monthly profit.

Again, I want to thank you for this opportunity and look forward to assisting you in making this company regain its strength and vitality.

Sincerely,

John P. Expert

CASE II

Knecht Roofing and Construction Company

You have met with Kevin Knecht and you know, following a quick look at what records he has, that he is in trouble—he has little cash, is barely up-to-date with his taxes and drives a big, fancy diesel truck. And while he does need a truck for his business, this one is unwarranted. His receipts are in a big storage box, although he uses a computer at times (his wife keeps the records) for compiling accounting information.

After a quick assessment, you realize that his business is in a bad way. He should be doing better because he has several current roofing projects. But if you do try to help him turn his business around, how would you be compensated? You need a new roof and you need it right now; maybe that is the best way to be compensated.

You agree to look at his records more thoroughly and advise Kevin how he can turn this business around. He knows there are big problems but he can't put his finger on them or make the necessary changes to increase profit. He is too busy right now performing the work—completing the roofing projects to which he is currently committed.

You agree to spend at least a half day each week or more working on Kevin's records and help Kevin make decisions that will turn the business around. It might take longer than 30 days.

You expect this will require a two-month time commitment—turnaround in one month and stabilization in the second. Kevin's commitment to you is that at the end of two months, he will re-roof your house in exchange for your services.

The benefits to Kevin are these:

- He will get a better look at his business through the records you are generating.

- He will get professional advice about much needed changes. Most importantly, he might be able to stay in business.

The benefits to you, the accountant and Profit Expert are:

- You will understand his business better, learn how to stabilize operations and possibly get a new roof out of the deal.
- He could become an ongoing write-up client. Kevin's wife is good at keeping the books. But right now, Kevin needs better than good; he needs solid, regular business advice.

Your risk is that Kevin will not have the working capital and other resources to work on your roof.

You and Kevin have a one-page letter of agreement (see next page) covering the turnaround project time as well as an additional ten or eleven months with you working as a consultant.

Dear Kevin,

It was a pleasure to meet with you yesterday to discuss the current condition of your business. I look forward to helping you determine how to make your business stronger.

Below is a brief description of the written agreement:

Project Work

As a profit and growth expert, during the next 30 days, I will focus on profit improvement strategies for your business. I will begin by assessing the position of your company and analyzing current business practices. I will then make recommendations for change, and then jointly, we will arrive at a plan that is comfortable for you and will accomplish your business objectives.

Outputs

Recently, your business has struggled to provide enough cash for operations as well as a reasonable income for your services. My hope is that with my help your business operations will provide sufficient cash for you to draw $1,000 per week without sacrificing operations.

Compensation

I look forward to being a valuable part of your management team. During the next several weeks I expect to devote at least 4 hours per week to this project. In return, we agreed that in two months you will replace the roof on my home. We can agree to specific terms at that time. At the end of the 30-day period, we will negotiate a longer-term business arrangement and create another written agreement if that seems appropriate.

Again, I want to thank you for the privilege of helping you strengthen your business.

Sincerely,

John P. Expert

CASE III
Sherwood's SureSave Market and Auto Repair

Sherwood's business has been so good for so long! It's hard to realize and accept the fact that things changed so quickly. The minute that new super-sized grocery store and convenient gas station opened across the street, business has been on the slide.

You have a good relationship with Tom and Scott and have been doing their accounting for years. Until now business has been good.

But things have changed. They need help. They need professional advice that you can provide because of your business and accounting expertise—you are a Profit Expert. And, you have some ideas that might help them grow their business, but you need to perform a thorough assessment before making recommendations.

They don't need another owner; they have cash in the bank albeit it is decreasing rapidly. They can pay you for your services, no problem.

Your commitment to them is to provide an assessment of the business situation and make recommendations as to what alternatives are viable for them. Then you will be the project manager, as required changes are implemented.

Their commitment to you is to pay your going rate, probably on a retainer basis, as they have been doing up to this point. You will also get a possible bonus based on how high additional profits become.

The benefits to the Sherwoods include:

- Development of a new business model to implement as they continue their profitable operations at this location.

- Get objective feedback of what is going on in their business and what they need to do to improve it.

And your benefits include:

- Provide you experience in using accounting information and geo-metric marketing concepts to develop a new business model.

- Develop new expertise with business problems where financial management is not the main issue.

This understanding was formalized in a one-page letter of agreement signed by all parties.

Dear Tom,

It was a pleasure meeting with you yesterday and discussing the current condition of your business, in particular, the eroding fuel sales. I look forward to helping you determine how to position your company to halt the resulting loss of profits.

Below is a brief description of our agreement:

Project Work

As a profit and growth expert, during the next 30 days I will focus on various marketing strategies. I will begin by assessing the position of your company and the local market place. After assessing the situation, I will make recommendations for change. Then, jointly, we will arrive at a plan that is comfortable for you and that will accomplish your business objectives.

Outputs

Although your business is financially strong, revenues are declining due to the recent competition caused by the opening of the grocery store across the street and its discounted gas prices. In a matter of weeks, based on current trends, your gas sales will be all but zero. To aid you, I will evaluate a number of different strategies designed to recover lost revenue. Once we jointly arrive at a reasonable solution, I will assist you through the design, test, and implementation steps.

Compensation

I look forward to being a valuable part of your management team for the next few weeks. I expect to devote around eight hours per week to this project. In return, I will charge you my customary management fee of $1,500 per month for the next 12 months. Once we have designed, tested, and implemented a reasonable solution, assuming you're satisfied with my assistance and the outcome, you will provide me with a $5,000 bonus.

Again, I want to thank you for the privilege of helping you reposition your business.

Sincerely,

John P. Expert

PART II – DEVELOP
WHAT NEEDS TO BE DONE?

The DEVELOP phase focuses on completing the business turn-around work. It is the second of three parts in our **Universal Project Management Model.** In the DISCOVERY phase you identified problems and set up the project. Now, in the DEVELOP phase, you are ready to dig in and get your hands dirty.

The DEVELOP phase covers Chapters Three through Eight and follows the Universal Turnaround Model, step-by-step, starting with assessing the current state of the business, developing a turnaround business plan, improving cash, reducing expenses, and improving revenue. The DEVELOP phase ends with a reassessment of the business at the end of the turnaround process. There is one chapter for each of the turnaround steps and each step represents one week in the six week turnaround process.

The assumption is that you have decided that this work is right for you, you want to develop your skills as a Profit Expert and a new written agreement is in place between you and the business owner. This agreement should be in place before you do any work or it probably will not ever be written.

The DOCUMENT phase, discussed in Chapter Nine, will record the major learning points—institutional wisdom—gleaned from the DISCOVER and DEVELOP phases.

THREE

STEP 1
Assessing the Situation

An assessment is a clear snapshot of where the business currently is. Objectives of an assessment include being able to describe the business's problems and deciding if business turnaround is probable or even possible in thirty days. If the decision is yes, then making profitable recommendations about necessary changes becomes another objective.

This chapter provides the knowledge and tools necessary to perform an objective assessment of the business and decide whether or not a turnaround is probable or even possible.

An assessment also gives you a chance to compare, or benchmark, what is happening in this business to what is happening in the industry. A benchmark is what the industry's present best-practices are currently.

The **Universal Turnaround Model** illustrates this first step in the turnaround process.

UNIVERSAL TURNAROUND MODEL

ACCOUNTING
INFORMATION

ADVISORY GROUP

INDUSTRY DATA

Some small business owners see only what they want to see. They are emotionally involved and live in a dream world, ignoring painful reality. But the business must be successful in more than just the owner's mind. As the Profit Expert you can be objective as you move through this first assessment step.

An accurate assessment includes an evaluation of three areas of the business:

People. This is a look at the people who are doing the work. Are the right people involved in the business and are they in the right positions?

Operations or procedures. This is usually called an operational audit and looks at the way things are done. What processes are used to complete the work?

Financial Statements. This includes an analysis of both the income statement and the balance sheet. What do the numbers tell you about the business?

Here's a closer look at all three areas of the assessment:

PEOPLE

Interviewing key employees is a great place to start—four or five people should be enough. This task is not as hard as you think. Keep in mind that there shouldn't be that many people to interview. People are generally very interesting and like to share their feelings about what is going on. You will uncover helpful information that can be used in completing this phase of the turnaround project just by talking to the people involved.

I have found that the best technique in asking questions is to start with general aspects of the business and then narrow the questions as you proceed. Some individuals don't need to be asked the broad questions because their only interest involves the day-to-day tasks.

There are some general questions that are helpful, more strategic if you will, that you can discuss with the owner. This information sets the context for any conversations you will have with other employees. The business owner can give you this information.

Not all questions are appropriate for all businesses; maybe none of them will be. Maybe just one of the questions will be important. The following list provides you with a place to start. Many times you are interviewing employees and performing an operational audit at the same time.

- *Tell me about your business?* (This is a great place to start.)
- *Why did you start the business?*
- *What should the business look like when it is successful?*
- *What is the business model (how the business makes money)?*
- *What is the gap between where the business is currently and what success looks like?*
- *Who are the key people?*
- *What is the marketing plan for the business?*

Learning about the business from interviews gives you an idea of what is happening before you look at the numbers. Some of the questions asked lead into or are part of the operational audit.

OPERATIONAL AUDIT

An operational audit is an evaluation of the way work gets done in this business. It could include a look at the following:

- Production processes
- Customer Service (from the customer's point of view)
- Competitors' benchmarks

Another way of looking at the business was introduced in my first book *In the BLACK: Nine Principles to Make Your Business Profitable.* The operational audit looks at the business's Marketing, Accounting and Production (MAP). I refer to this as MAPping a business, or examining those three critical operational areas of a small business. The result is the same; you want to get a good picture of what is currently happening in the business.

PERTINENT QUESTIONS FOR THE OPERATIONAL AUDIT

The key to good consulting is not having all the right answers; it's having the right questions. I have found the three questions below are a great way to start any business conversation:

What is working well?

What is not working so well?

What changes are needed to make the business profitable?

Make a table with three columns, one column for each of the questions, and start talking to people. These questions are excellent in a general sense. They are noninvasive and nonthreatening. The information compiled just through these general questions can lead to some amazing findings and effective recommendations.

In many cases, more specific questions may be appropriate. Here are some that I have found to be effective. You would never ask one person all these questions. Some may be more pertinent than others given the situation. Use the ones that work for you.

What does the industry look like?

Read the trade journals and whatever else you can find to ascertain where the industry is going. If the future is bleak, it's better to know now rather than after investing a lot more time and capital into a sinking ship.

What is the current economic situation with the industry and location?

The business world changes daily. Adapting to change is the key to continued business growth.

What is the company's unique selling proposition?

A century ago having a unique selling proposition was not a consideration—location was the key to a company's success. People went to a company simply for convenience, not because they were better than everyone else. They chose the grocery store, dentist, and blacksmith based on the number of steps from their doorstep to the location of the business regardless of whether they liked or disliked their experience once they got there.

Today, the world is flat, and competition can come from anywhere in the world. You need to communicate why your business is unique from everyone else's. If you don't, you won't grow.

If you are competing on price alone, WAL*MART would be a very tough competitor. If you are adding service or value, then you could be very successful.

How long does it take from lead to sale on average? Or what does the sales cycle look like?

Turnaround options for companies with long sales-lead times are different from businesses that depend on walk-in traffic for their revenue. For instance, imagine that the average sales cycle is one month from lead to sale. This involves more time commitment from the business staff and more potential for a lost sale. If you shave 50% off the lead time by sharing a special offer or by maintaining contact, this would likely not only shorten the sales cycle, but also increase sales.

Who are the employees and what skills do they bring to the business?

Do an inventory of your employees—they are the company's most valuable asset. If some of them are idle or not up to the task, you're not doing anyone a favor by keeping them. Instead, you're harming those that are doing a great job.

It's often been said, hire slow and fire fast. This is even truer when the business is struggling than when it's doing well.

What is the turnover rate for the employees?

A high turnover rate can bury a company. If the company you're working with can't hold onto a qualified work force, they're doing something wrong.

My experience at Universal Accounting Center is that to replace an employee, the cost averages about a third of the annual salary when considering the time and expense spent advertising and interviewing candidates. At minimum wage that would be over $4,000.

Once an employee is on staff for six months or more, it's estimated that the cost to replace the employee is equal to 1-2 times his annual salary. This comes in two ways: 1) the cost to retrain, and 2) the lost opportunity. This doesn't even consider the fact that the lost employee was a known entity—the new person may or may not be as good as the one being replaced.

Although research findings vary, my observation is that the national turnover rate is about 20%. Many industries have turnover rates much higher than that. Some construction companies experience up to 30% turnover rate and some CPA firms average 50%. Expect and accept turnover irrespective of your industry.

At this point in time, you should have a good operational picture of what the small business looks like. You have met the key employees and know the key processes that are followed on a daily and weekly basis.

What roadblocks prohibit this business from turning around?

To evaluate what roadblocks exist, ask yourself what prevents this business from growing. Then divide these into two categories: internal roadblocks and external roadblocks. You have the most control over internal roadblocks as they can be further categorized as organizational and financial.

Internal factors may include employee morale and skill level (including management), capital limitations, time constraints, idle capacity, poor collections history, and inadequate sales strategy.

For instance, if your cash flow is a major barrier to your growth, you may wish to consider alternative financing, sharing equity, or contacting vendors for lengthened terms.

If you are dependent upon walk-in sales, location and front appeal are key considerations for your business. I'm amazed at how many businesses I walk into or drive by that have allowed the front of their business to become dirty and weedy. If you don't care about how your business looks to the public, you're fighting a losing battle when it comes to walk-in traffic.

What if capacity restricts you? One restaurant had a great location, was well known, and filling every table every evening. They knew that with some more dining space they could substantially increase their revenues, but they didn't want to start all over again in a new neighborhood. So, they got the necessary permits to expand onto the sidewalk.

External factors can be more difficult to overcome. You may be in a market where adequately trained individuals are in short supply. One client couldn't get motivated, adequately trained telemarketers to cover inbound phone calls. They moved their call center to a college town just 50 miles from their operations and found all the eager, skilled telephone sales people needed.

Is lack of response to advertising methods internal or external? It could be both. For instance, if you are using the wrong message or the wrong media, you have full control making the change; you just need to determine which is working and which is not. However, these are also both external factors as your target market may also be changing, which means you have to understand what's causing them to change. This requires constant surveying.

If the industry is dropping, you must understand why and determine future expectations. The Internet is a great source for articles that will bring you up-to-date with the experts.

Who are the competitors and how are they doing?

If everyone in the industry is struggling, then many of the barriers are external. This doesn't mean you should give up and run. It can mean just the opposite. Unless you are selling typewriters or sewing machines, consider the fact that most industries experience normal cycles.

The companies that survive know how to adapt, and many of them come out stronger because they are leaner and smarter. Furthermore, opportunities to get better deals on supplies from the vendors exist (they're probably struggling as well), and you can draw customers away from the competition as they become leery of their former vendors.

How old is the business?

You've probably heard that half the businesses fail in the first year. Of those who survive their first anniversary, only half will enjoy their fifth. And of those, only half will enjoy their first decade. That means about 90% won't make it ten years. What is it that has kept this business going for this long?

If the business is new, they have a lot to learn and likely don't have the survivalist attitude down yet. They'll be less inclined to make the changes the business needs, especially if it involves pain or difficulty.

What natural business alliances does the business have?

Every industry has natural business alliances with other industries. For example, the real estate agent is a natural ally of mortgage agencies, remodeling contractors, title shops, insurance agents, and home inspection companies.

A building contractor should know sub-contractors, building supply vendors, and real estate agents.

Who else does the business owner need to know?

There's a core of professionals that every business owner needs to have on his Rolodex who are eagerly awaiting the opportunity to help. This includes an accountant, a lawyer, a banker, and a business insurance agent. You're the accountant, but how about the others?

What experience does the business owner have?

This might not apply at this particular time. According to Michael Gerber, author of the *E-Myth* book series, most businesses are started by a technician having an entrepreneurial seizure. This means that the business owner knew how to do something, but it likely wasn't running a business. So, most learn it through the school of hard-knocks or give up before they get their degree. If you were giving out a letter grade, where would you put this person:

A — The owner has a sound understanding of financial concepts, is comfortable speaking with bankers, and understands EVERYTHING you tell him. Bankruptcy is never an option.

B — The owner can read a financial statement and recognizes the value of keeping track of money. He is conscientious about paying bills on time and anticipates money problems before it's too late. Bankruptcy is only spoken with the attorney and never without a tear in his eye.

C — The owner calls the bank every morning to find out what the balance is. The main indication of a prosperous/failing business is the amount of money in the account. He thinks: "What's the worst thing that can happen? Bankruptcy? I can live with that."

D — The owner figures that as long as he has checks, then they're in good shape. One or two bounced checks a month is a good month. The bankruptcy attorney's card is in the owner's Rolodex.

F — The bankruptcy attorney's number is on the owner's speed dial.

This rating system can be used with all key employees of the business. It can help you get a better feeling for the business, and if some employees need to be terminated, then it might help with that difficult task.

FINANCIAL AUDIT

An examination of the financial statements and accounting records is next on the agenda. The accounting information is critically important as you will see throughout this book. Accounting ratios are valuable and deserve time in the assessment phase of the project and re-examination throughout the rest of the project.

The assumption is that your expertise is in this financial audit section. The focus is on the bigger picture and on major questions that you should be addressing. In some small businesses, one transaction can change some accounting ratios dramatically.

FINANCIAL ANALYSIS

I'm amazed when I watch crime shows on television how much is learned from the most insignificant item at the crime scene. Similarly, it's amazing how much you can learn from a thorough analysis of the financial statements. In most cases, the financial analysis is completed by you alone or with the bookkeeper's help if there is one.

Without financial data, it's all guess work. You'll make suggestions that will lack substance and direction, both of which are needed to provide confidence in the outcome.

If the business lacks financial statements, you're best served creating them from whatever information is available. If you've never done this before, enlist the help of someone who has.

There are two types of reviews:

- Trend analysis: Financial statements change over time. Anomalies and changes in procedures become evident when you compare periods side by side.

- Indexing: Using ratios and financial indicators identify strengths and weaknesses that wouldn't be obvious otherwise. This becomes invaluable when you compare the indices to the company's peers or with industry benchmarks.

What has been the history of the company's bank account balance?

Cash is simply an asset, like inventory and equipment. It's to protect and use wisely. If the bank balance takes more spikes and dips than the Rocky Mountains, the business could be out of control.

What is the condition of the company's Accounts Receivable aging?

Ask a small business owner if he will collect all of his accounts receivable and he's likely to tell you "of course." Unless there's a mirror behind him, you probably didn't notice him crossing his fingers. The fact is that the numbers won't lie, and any receivable over 90 days past due is unlikely to ever be collected.

Run the report and find out what the real story is.

Have there been significant changes in category percentages over the last six months?

Your software makes this really easy. Simply print out a monthly or quarterly P&L with the percentages of sales to the side. Then, look for anomalies or problematic trends. Obviously, some of the percentage changes may be inconsequential among small expense categories —look for big-dollar changes that have put the company in peril.

List the ratios—how are they calculated and what is expected? Incidentally, lowering current liabilities has a larger impact on the current ratio than an equal increase in current assets.

Have sales revenues and quantities sold gone down? Why?

A picture is worth a thousand words. Better yet, a graph. I prefer to look at sales on a quarterly basis as opposed to monthly. Graph the revenues and quantities separately. If pricing hasn't changed dramatically, they will usually follow each other. However, if you can see a major difference in the slope and trend of the two, it says that your prices have fluctuated.

Observe the long-term direction of the sales. Has the change been slow or were there some major dips. If you can see dramatic changes, find out what happened during those periods. If the line is straight or horizontal, then you need to look at external factors that may be causing that situation, such as competitive pressures, economic changes, etc.

What advertising methods have been used in the past? What has worked and what hasn't?

Pick up any marketing book and you will learn valuable marketing strategies. The problem is that you might have tried several of the strategies and they haven't worked. In fact, you may have tried them several times (every time you picked up a marketing book or talked with a marketing consultant) and they still didn't work. Find out what has really worked in the past

What is the average cost to buy/sell a unit?

If you buy and sell inventory, this equation at first consideration is an easy one. But, stop. What about the cost of the purchasing agent, the cost of the person stocking the inventory, the cost of the clerk selling the item, and the cost to account and collect the sale? All of a sudden you may realize that there's a reason you're not drinking pina coladas on the Riviera. This analysis can usually be done by you alone.

What is the average markup?

So many owners start a business with no idea of what markup they should be charging. They're sometimes amazed and astonished to learn that the most common markup is 100%. (Cost of purchase x 200% = Selling price.)

Once you know the markup for the company you may compare it to the industry average (the suppliers will tell you what your competition is charging). Make sure you're in the ball park.

Also be aware that the markup tells you how much you can spend to get an incremental sale. For instance, if you markup a product that cost you $500 at 100%, then you're pricing it at $1,000. You can afford to spend $500 to get one more sale. What if you know an out-of-work salesman that would walk door-to-door eight hours per day to sell your product for a commission of $250 each? Should you do it? What if he could sell two per day? He'd be on cloud nine, and you'd be somewhere on cloud eight.

What is their monthly, weekly, and daily break even?

Drill down to what needs to be accomplished today just to cover costs. You do this by calculating your annual or monthly breakeven, then dividing that number by the average number of work days (260 annually, 21.7 monthly). Multiply that product by five to get the weekly breakeven.

Let's first look at the sample break-even analysis again. The assumption is that this is a weekly breakeven chart.

	Sales	$ 50,000
Minus	Variable Costs	$ 20,000
Equals	Gross Profit Margin	$ 30,000
Divided by	Units Sold	3,000
Equals	Gross Profit Margin per Unit	$ 10
	Fixed Costs	$ 15,000
Divided by	Gross Profit Margin per Unit	$ 10
Equals	Breakeven Units	1,500

Now, determine if it's reasonable to expect those results every day or every week, and what is needed to achieve that. This data should be in the accounting information of the business.

What are the lending sources?

The business owner may have already tried to get financing unsuccessfully for whatever reason, and may feel there's no hope. But, they may not have ever heard of factoring receivables or of selling their assets to a leasing company for some quick cash, then leasing them back. How about an SBA loan or borrowing from a credit union? There's more than one way to skin a cat.

What interest rates are being paid?

Interest on loans and payables is one of your most negotiable debts. Banks and suppliers will lower the interest rate quickly if they feel it will help get the debt paid. This even includes commercial loans that are tied to prime. Let these vendors and banks know that you are experiencing difficulties, and that you plan on paying the debt but the current interest is killing the business. Ask them if they can drop a point, or even three. It may not end up saving the business, but every little bit helps.

Furthermore, if you know what debts are carrying the highest percentage of interest, you address those particular debts first.

What is the company's current credit rating?

There's nothing in the short-term you can do to alter this, but it will help you know what your options are. If the credit score is above 700, then financing is in your future. If it's in the 400's or below, you can kiss financing good bye.

How do I compare my client's business to peer businesses?

Of course there's an easy way and a hard way to do this. First, the hard way: The RMA (Risk Management Associates) releases abstracts of financial indices by industry. This book (and others like it) is probably available at your local library. They will provide you with average results from other companies in your client's industry and of a similar size so that you can see how you compare. In most cases, if your client's company is struggling, you can locate one or more areas where the company compares poorly to its peers, and then begin determining what improvements need to occur.

UNIVERSAL BUSINESS ANALYSIS TOOL

Now the easy way.

When interviews, operational analysis and financial analysis are complete, software can be used to further analyze financial information.

Analysis is easy when you work with Universal Accounting Center. With an income statement and balance sheet, you can provide assessment reports of any business, comparing it to peer companies by size in its industry.

Universal Accounting Center can provide a complete, detailed report showing how a given company compares to its peer companies. It is a simple process of providing summarized information to Universal. Within 3 business days we will email you a complete report showing the businesses' successes and failings, together with recommendations of where changes need to be made.

- **9 ratios are in accounting**
- **5 ratios are in marketing**
- **5 are in production**

With the assessment nearly complete, the last steps include compiling the information, such as strengths and weaknesses, you have gathered in some meaningful way.

Other commercially offered assessments are available. The message is that great software is available to help with business assessments.

ASSESSMENT RESULTS

At the end of this step you should have the following information:

- A clear description of the current business situation.

- A decision that a business turnaround is possible. You need to agree that the turnaround process is doable. Make sure your agreement with the owner is still valid. This is a perfect time to ensure the owner is still committed to the one-year agreement.

- A list of recommendations that can be quickly implemented in order to stabilize the business. In the planning chapter that follows, these recommendations will be prioritized and implementation planned in more detail.

This assessment step is critical. If the general consensus is that the business cannot survive the next 30 days, even with your best efforts, then the best alternative is to close the business as quickly as possible. If the business could become viable upon applying recommended changes, then proceed to the planning phase where you will write and implement a turnaround business plan, which will include those recommendations.

Once you've had a chance to look over the data, you'll want to discuss issues with the owner to fill in the gaps and to understand more about the business structure and organization.

Frequently Asked Questions

What information do I need to perform an assessment?

To begin with, you need access to key employees and financial statements. If possible you want the entire financial file—not just paper reports. You want to be able to look for trends, and details that wouldn't come through last year's copy of the balance sheet and income statement.

What outside research needs to be completed?

The more information you get, the better, at least to a point. You need to turn this business around quickly. You don't have time to read everything you can find— that could take weeks of intensive study. But, with the help of the Internet, you can learn a lot in a short time. Review available trade journals. The SBA has some terrific resources, as well as other Internet sites.

How do I keep from jumping to conclusions prematurely?

Chances are that your first assumption will be wrong. If it were that easy your client would have already figured it out. For that reason you must go through all the steps of assessment before you start formulating recommendations. It's also a good idea to review the data you've found as well as your suggestions with someone else whose judgment you respect.

How do I keep from getting lost in the details?

We accountants love numbers to a fault. We've been known to spend eight hours figuring out why we're ten cents short on the bank reconciliation. What a loss!

One way I've found to keep from worrying about details is to round everything to thousands (I usually show tenths of thousands). Then, if the magazine subscriptions were up $40 from year to year, I'll never lose any sleep over it.

How much math do I need to understand?

Other than basic arithmetic, you'll need to be able to solve simple algebraic problems. For instance, you may want to know how much you need to change one variable to achieve a certain result. For instance, if your industry has a current ratio (current assets divided by current liabilities) of 1.6, and your business is at 0.7, how much would you need to increase your current assets (or lower your current liabilities) to match your peers?

What software and tools do I need to perform the assessment?

Accounting software is a nice start. Beyond that, you will need a spreadsheet and word processing software. You will want a calculator, a fax machine, and a printer for your computer (which I assume you already have).

If you're a student of the Universal Professional Bookkeeper Program, check out the instruction given in Module 3. It will lead you through the process.

Without experience, completing an accurate assessment can be very difficult. For that reason, I recommend using a professional assessment software tool like the one we use at Universal Accounting Center and described on page 82. This chapter discusses various options. However, the process described in Chapter Three is complete, so a professional tool is unnecessary.

SUMMARY—WHERE YOU SHOULD BE AT THIS POINT

You should have a good picture of the business (strengths, weaknesses, opportunities and threats), a decision that business stabilization is achievable, and a list of recommendations for implementation.

You and the business owner have decided the business can be turned around and critical people have agreed to move ahead into the planning phase. Possibly you will rewrite your agreement with the owner. The assessment may show other things about the business that need your involvement.

You have visited with key employees and have completed an operational audit. You have also examined the financial statements thoroughly. Usually, you can complete this assessment by yourself. The financial audit should include a breakeven analysis.

The time allotted for this assessment is five days—the first five days of the turnaround period. Many are tempted to take action before knowing what is happening in the business. This assessment is a critical first step in the turnaround process.

CHAPTER THREE
ASSESSING THE SITUATION
Key Learning Points

- A clear and accurate assessment of what is currently happening in the business is a critical first step of the turnaround project. This assessment comes from your analysis of the financial statements, an analysis of the operations within the business and interviews with several key employees. From this analysis, you have developed a list of the business's strengths and weaknesses.

  The result of your analysis is a list of recommendations and action steps for a quick business turnaround. Recommendations can only be made after an accurate assessment is performed.

- Interviewing skills, including asking the right questions, are important in gaining valuable information. The assessment is not an ominous task—it can be done simply with the right questions and the right information.

- Software is available for assessing the financial information of the business.

CASE I
Miriam's Art and Frame Shop

After just eight hours, you have learned (based on your accountant's training), a great deal more about Miriam's business than you knew before. Probably, the most startling: There is evidence that her office manager has been stealing from her. You don't know how much yet, but thus far you have found several checks that were obviously written by the office manager to pay her personal bills (she didn't do a lot to cover it up). You suspect it adds up to tens of thousands of dollars. You had rarely been to the business before because the office manager always brought company records to you.

You have noted that her children have charged extensively against the company credit cards, and because they aren't employees, the purchases are personal, not business-related.

Other important insights include the lack of correlation between her sales and payroll. In other words, her sales fluctuate wildly, but her payroll remains flat.

Inventory is a major concern. Miriam buys more than she needs and saves the left-over pieces. These require more and more storage space.

This assessment phase has taught you a lot about Miriam's Art and Frame Shop. After reviewing her ratios compared to other businesses in her industry of approximately the same size, you have noted the following strengths and weaknesses:

Strengths:

- She has plenty of customers.
- She has viable products and services.
- She has good working conditions.

Weaknesses:

- Cash and expenses are out of control.
- Sales and payroll do not correlate.
- Credit card use by family members is out of control.
- Employee theft is occurring.

From your estimation the business is viable. You know you can help her, but she needs to make quick changes to ensure continued success. **Cash is the big problem.** People are stealing from her, expenses are responsible in some areas and high in others, and inventory seems excessive compared to revenue. Miriam may also need some marketing help when the focus turns to increasing revenue. However, the potential for improvement is here.

Turnaround project work will focus on these things:

- Getting cash under control.
- Getting expenses under control, including inventory.
- Optimizing payroll costs to more closely correlate with sales.
- Turn to marketing enhancement when expenses are under control.

Miriam's Financial Statements through the last 12 months.

ANNUAL INCOME STATEMENT

Sales	291,200
Cost of Goods Sold	116,480
GROSS PROFIT	174,720
Advertising	7,200
Automobile	3,000
Depreciation	6,000
Payroll	99,840
Rent	18,000
Supplies	3,000
Other	0
TOTAL EXPENSES	137,040
NET INCOME	37,680

ANNUAL BALANCE SHEET

Cash	2,250
Accounts Receivable	15,000
Inventory	12,000
Fixed Assets	35,000
TOTAL ASSETS	64,250
Accounts Payable	10,000
Other Liabilities	19,000
Equity	(2,430)
Net Income	37,680
TOTAL LIABILITIES AND EQUITY	64,250

CASE II

Knecht Roofing and Construction

Fortunately, Kevin has been paying his taxes and is current through the end of last year. However, he is behind on this year's taxes.

As you put together the financial records for this year, you notice a whole lot of money going out. Until recently, Kevin has been drawing out at least $1,000 a week from the business, putting a strain on the cash account. And he has a lot of expensive toys at home requiring monthly payments.

Expenses are out of control compared to the amount of work he has coming in. In many cases, his expenses are higher than what he bid on the job. There may be some tax problems as well, but that is a problem for another day. Your immediate concern is stabilizing the business.

To make matters worse, Kevin has recently cut back on the number of jobs he is taking on; he is turning down work. You suspect it is because he is a little discouraged.

This is really a margin problem; he is charging well below market for his jobs. Right now his average cost and expenses per job are $3,600 while his revenue for those same jobs averages $3,400. This is before his $1,000 a week draw. This will not keep him in business for very long. It's a good thing that his wife works. His bids or his margins need to increase—or both! He may not win every bid, but he has a good reputation so he will get the work needed to be profitable.

From this early assessment, strengths and areas of improvement have been identified:

Strengths:

- Kevin does great work.
- He has plenty of jobs and has a great back log of work ahead of him.
- Kevin has a good reputation among contractors.

Weaknesses:

- Cash is short.
- Kevin's weekly draw is hurting his cash position.
- Margins on jobs are not high enough to sustain a viable business.

The turnaround project work will focus on these areas:

- Monitoring expenses more effectively and getting them under control.
- Increasing margins on construction jobs. This includes the bidding process and better management of expenses.
- Controlling cash more effectively.
- Breakeven is two jobs per week where now he is averaging less than that. He needs three jobs a week to take a draw.

Knecht's Financial Statements through the last 12 months.

ANNUAL INCOME STATEMENT

Sales	262,000
Cost of Goods Sold	187,500
GROSS PROFIT	74,500
Advertising	3,600
Automobile	12,000
Depreciation	14,000
Payroll	40,000
Rent	6,000
Supplies	6,000
Other	
TOTAL EXPENSES	81,600
NET INCOME	(7,100)

ANNUAL BALANCE SHEET

Cash	1,250
Accounts Receivable	4,000
Inventory	0
Fixed Assets	70,000
TOTAL ASSETS	75,250
Accounts Payable	12,000
Other Liabilities	52,000
Equity	18,350
New Income	(7,100)
TOTAL LIABILITIES and Equity	75,250

CASE III

Sherwood's SureSave Market and Auto Repair

Sherwood's had very strong financial statements until the previous six months, which correlated with the opening of the big grocery store across the street. Since then gasoline volume and the number of customers visiting the convenience store plummeted.

Management is good. The auto repair business has great margins. Expenses are under control. An assessment of the past will not be too helpful here, except to ascertain that they were doing a good job in record keeping.

The big need right now is improving revenue to replace what has been lost to the new grocery store across the street. The business model, which worked for so many years, no longer works! A new model for making money is needed. Sherwood's is seeing a10% erosion in gasoline sales every week.

Historical financial statements provide much information on sales trends and cost patterns. Your assessment enables you to determine the following:

Strengths	**Weaknesses**
• Strong cash position.	• Strong competition from neighboring business.
• Great location for something and they own the buildings.	• Marketing location.
• Good management.	• Revenue losses (gasoline) are growing every week.
• Loyal customer base in auto repair shop.	• Current business model no longer works.
• Adequate expense control.	

The focus is on product and service changes. A new business model needs to be designed and implemented that will work in the changing neighborhood environment. They know what a profitable company looks like and how to manage one effectively. Now they must create a new one quickly.

An advisory group would be very helpful for Sherwood's at this time. The internal workings are under control but new marketing ideas are greatly needed. New ideas may come from outsiders. The manager of the new grocery store across the street could be a very interesting member of that advisory group.

Sherwood's Financial Statements through the last 12 months.

ANNUAL INCOME STATEMENT

Sales 1,020,000
Cost of Goods Sold 650,000

GROSS PROFIT 370,000

Advertising 50,400
Automobile 5,000
Depreciation 25,000
Payroll 180,000
Rent 0
Supplies 4,000
Other

TOTAL EXPENSES 264,400

NET INCOME 105,600

ANNUAL BALANCE SHEET

Cash 40,600
Accounts Receivable 0
Inventory 70,000
Fixed Assets 550,000

TOTAL ASSETS 660,600

Accounts Payable 50,000
Other Liabilities 325,000
Equity 180,000
Net Income 105,600

TOTAL LIABILITIES 660,600
AND EQUITY

FOUR

STEP 2
Planning the Turnaround Project

The assessment phase is about gathering all kinds of pertinent information to get the big picture of what is happening in the business. Change recommendations have been generated; the decision has been confirmed that the business can be stabilized and the business owner is committed to the changes.

This planning step takes the assessment information and more importantly, the recommendations for profitable change and creates a turnaround business plan—the written guide you will follow during the turnaround process.

Small business owners tend to be doers, not planners! Writing a turnaround business plan is not at the top of their priority list. Verbal communication is important in communicating to all concerned what is happening but a written document is critical in ensuring that everyone gets exactly the same message, especially after a few weeks of hard work in turning the business around.

This second step is illustrated in the **Universal Turnaround Model** on the following page:

You, as the Profit Expert, **UNIVERSAL TURNAROUND MODEL** are the professional presence during the analyzing and planning phases. You completed a solid assessment of the business and those findings and recommendations should be summarized on one or two pages. With you and the business owner working

together, a turnaround business plan can be developed quickly and should be no longer than four pages.

The result of the assessment is a list of recommendations and potential action steps. The table below illustrates how recommendations can be sorted and prioritized.

RECOMMENDATION EVALUATION GRID

The Recommendation Evaluation Grid allows you to prioritize recommendations made in the previous assessment chapter. The table has four quadrants used to sort recommendations by control and impact. The most important recommendations are those with high impact on business results where you or the business owner have high control.

RECOMMENDATION EVALUATION GRID

	High Control	Low Control
High Impact	1	2
Low Impact	3	4

For example, during the Assessment Phase of the turnaround project, strengths, weaknesses, opportunities and threats were evaluated. Recommendations for needed changes were developed. Many times more recommendations are made than can be adequately implemented during the turnaround period. This evaluation grid sorts those change recommendations into workable priorities.

The vertical axis rates the impact of the recommendation and the horizontal axis rates the control you have over the action step. High priority recommendations or changes will gravitate toward Quadrant 1 where both the impact on the business and internal control are high.

All recommended changes are evaluated with each recommended change placed in the quadrant where it makes the most sense. Recommendations in Quadrant 1 are those of the highest priority to execute. That is because these recommendations have a high impact on the business and can be highly controlled.

Here is the process:

1. List all recommended changes.

2. Sort them into the four quadrants.

3. Focus on action steps that gravitate toward Quadrant 1.

4. Prioritize Quadrant I action steps by impact.

The resulting list of action steps are things having high impact on the business and over which you have high control. These recommendations will also probably fit into one of three areas of focus in our turnaround: improving cash management, reducing expenses or increasing revenue. These categories will be addressed in the subsequent three chapters.

Here's an example: What if nobody is tracking the bank account? Suppose the business sells heavy equipment, and lower bank interest rates would help you make more sales, in fact, maybe a lot more sales. The impact of that change would be high. But, unfortunately, our control over what happens to interest rates is very low. Thus, that recommendation would fall into quadrant 2.

Here's another example: The business's cash accounts need to be managed more effectively. You are unsure whether the cash is spent wisely and if adequate controls are in place. In a turnaround situation, the impact of that recommendation is high as is the business's internal control. This recommendation would make it into Quadrant 1 and would probably be one of the first recommended changes addressed by the turnaround team.

TURNAROUND BUSINESS PLANS

Business plans can be long and detailed. That is not our purpose here. Time is precious so the Turnaround Business Plan cannot be too involved. There is a need, however, to have something written down, perhaps no longer than two to four pages. This document states the urgency, the vision, and the results needed to quickly turn the business around.

It is the "manual," so to speak, for the turnaround process even though more detailed tactics will develop in subsequent phases. It also sets the tone for an agreement—a rallying cry around success, more sales, more satisfied customers, etc.

These plans should not take long to complete but are critical in assuring that everyone involved in the turnaround project knows what is expected. Most often, the process of developing a business plan is even more valuable than the document itself.

PROFIT EXPERT INVOLVEMENT

Probably you, as the Profit Expert, are the main architect of this Turnaround Business Plan. The action steps you recommend will focus on Quadrant 1 recommendation in the Recommendations Evaluation Grid. The resources in the middle of the Universal Turnaround Model can again be a very important source of information in turn-around planning.

This entire project can keep you as busy as you want. That is why it is important to ensure you are adequately compensated. You are in the best position to create the Turnaround Business Plan, so you might as well do it yourself. You know or have access to critical information about the business; you have completed the assessment yourself.

BUSINESS OWNER INVOLVEMENT

The business owner must be involved as much as possible in the planning process. They are surely interested in the survival and turn-around of their business. Their weakness is your strength—you can be the project manager for both the planning process and the actual turnaround steps. However, it is important to realize that the more the owner is involved in creating the plan and the specific recom-mendations necessary to achieve the desired results, the more he will support the implementation of that plan. People support what they help create.

ADVISORY GROUP AND TURNAROUND BUSINESS PLAN

This is a good time to organize the Advisory Group if you haven't done so already. This is the third major resource that will provide you with critical accounting information and industry data, around which the **Universal Turnaround Model** exists. It could be that the owner wants nothing to do with an Advisory Group because he doesn't feel comfortable sharing information with outsiders about his business, especially when it is struggling. The Advisory Group should only be organized with the owner's permission.

This Advisory Group is beneficial in brainstorming ideas about how to turn around the business. Here are suggestions in creating an effective Advisory Group:

- The group should comprise no more than five and no less than three people. I suggest you select experts in production, marketing, sales—people who will complement your skills as well as the owner's—perhaps a customer or an attorney.
- You, as the accountant, should be the chairperson.
- Consider selecting a banker or someone with an objective view, who is not emotionally involved with the business.

The complementary strengths of different members working together as a team will enable you to consider all aspects of business from diverse perspectives. Together, the group should have a wide variety of experience and expertise. The group's goal is providing wisdom and counsel in making operational decisions. You can benchmark your ideas against theirs.

The owner may be opposed to working with an Advisory Group because of the sensitivity of information shared. If that is the case, explain to the owner that valuable insight is gained from this group if used correctly. However, the owner has the final say in all decisions, including whether or not there will be an Advisory Group.

How do you ask people to be part of an Advisory Group? How can you get them together? And how often?

A simple way of gathering potential group members is to invite them to lunch, perhaps not all at once but one or two at a time. Lunch is a great way to get inexpensive information. Brainstorming with the

Advisory Group about what can be done to turn things around is the purpose of this lunch activity.

You might have to pay some of them for their time and expertise. That's okay. If you are paying an expert $200 per hour for $1,000's worth of information, you see a substantial return on your investment. The information can have a tremendous impact on the business turnaround.

If lunch doesn't work, a formal meeting held during the day or evening may work just as well. Given that this turnaround situation is happening quickly, it might be that you only have the opportunity to meet with them once. After that, phone calls to individual group members may suffice.

TURNAROUND BUSINESS PLAN OUTLINE

Planning is based on the base business, moving into other marketing quadrants from there. (See the marketing model in Chapter Seven.) The base business and the base business model are the key success factors in the turnaround.

The planning process should follow the business outline below. It is sequential in order, thus making it easy to follow both in creation and implementation. If the Business Plan is four pages maximum, it can't be too detailed.

The goal is to have a very short, power-packed guide to use as a foundation for all decisions in the next four weeks. Below is a business plan outline. Actual examples of our three cases are included at the end of this chapter.

Description of situation

• Symptoms

• Problem Statements

• Opportunities and Risks

Business Model

- How does the business make money right now?
- How will the business make money in the future?
- What does success look like?

Major changes needed to make the new business model successful

- Turnaround Project Objective
- Resources needed to make the change
- Time plan for the next 4 weeks to reach turnaround
- What resources do you have access to right now and what will you need from all sources to make the implementation of this plan successful?

Operations Plan

- Managing Cash
- Reducing Expenses
- Increasing Revenue

People

- Who are the right people to turn the business around?
- What will each of them do?
- Who should be in the Advisory Group?
- How will the owner be involved?
- How will you as the accountant be involved? What will your role be in the decision-making process?

Universal Score Card

- A Score Card is a one-page report which captures critical information on a weekly basis that needs to be constantly monitored. The measurements might be different in every turnaround situation. As was learned in the Hawthorne studies of the 1920's and 1930's, what is monitored, improves. That is the purpose of the Score Card—monitoring critical data on a weekly basis so you can see progress made in the turnaround project.

- Your role as an accountant may be the compilation of this information, but is certainly the interpretation of the information for the owner, who will then be assured the process is working.

An example of a Score Card is illustrated below.

UNIVERSAL SCORE CARD MODEL (EXAMPLE)

Description	Week 1 Assessment	Week 2 Planning	Week 3 Cash	Week 4 Expenses	Week 5 Revenue	Week 6 Reassess	Target
Cash in the bank							
Accounts Receivable over 30/90 days old							
Bills (cash) owed in the next week							
End of Month Accounting ratios							
Weekly Sales							
Monthly Sales							
Cash sales vs. Credit							
Number of jobs							
Revenue per job							

This is an example of a Universal Score Card that can be used in almost any small business. It should be monitored on a weekly basis. Targets are in the far right-hand column.

The Universal Score Card provides weekly indications of how the business is doing, particularly as it proceeds in this turnaround effort. Targets generated during the planning phase are inserted in the far right hand column. Comparisons are then made on a weekly basis between actual and targets to ascertain what progress is being made.

Accounting information is critical in forming the Universal Score Card. Almost all the information on the Universal Score Card is developed somewhere within the accounting system. You, as the accountant, are the expert in providing information and interpreting it correctly to help the owner make sound business decisions during this turnaround project and thereafter.

Frequently Asked Questions

How detailed should the Turnaround Business Plan be?

As detailed as needed, but four pages maximum. The roles and responsibilities need clear definition. The Score Card needs to be comprehensive so that you can accurately monitor progress. The recommendations and action steps must be as thorough as possible making sense to all involved.

Is this Turnaround Business Plan worth a week's time?

Yes. The better you plan at this stage, the more effective your implementation will be.

Is an Advisory Group really necessary?

Probably not in all cases. But, it sure is beneficial in evaluating ideas and expanding your network of local business people. Some of the questions this group might address include:

- Is a turnaround or even stabilization achievable? What are realistic expectations?
- Can it be done quickly enough to save the business?
- Does the turnaround still seem doable with these action steps in place?
- Does the business have long-term viability? Our focus is on the next 30 days. But what can be accomplished in 60 days? In 90?

How do you mentally prepare for this turnaround process?

No easy answer here. *Red to Black in 30 Days* provides the models and processes; you already have accounting expertise. Mental toughness comes from experience and commitment to turnaround goals as well as your commitment growing your own accounting practice.

SUMMARY – WHERE YOU SHOULD BE AT THIS POINT

The Business Turnaround Plan is complete; it is important to ensure the business owner agrees with everything written and is *committed* to the changes. If he was unwilling to take your advice and recommendations but more-or-less agreed to move on with the process, that might be evidence that he will not follow the action steps outlined in the business plan.

If the business owner cannot find the time to be involved sufficiently in the assessment or planning processes, then he might not be committed to the changes necessary. Some of these proposed changes could be very difficult for him to implement, particularly if it involves changing people or eliminating people who are friends, family members, or have been with him for a long time or since the beginning of the business.

You have assessed and planned and are now well into the DEVELOP phase. The timetable is set. The roles and responsibilities are established. The resources are currently in place or soon will be in place. Accounting, production, and marketing must show potential improvements for the turnaround to take place.

CHAPTER FOUR
PLANNING THE TURNAROUND PROJECT
Key Learning Points

- A written turnaround business plan (1 to 4 pages) is the guide for the remainder of the turnaround project. It is important to have that guiding document in writing so that everyone's recollections and expectations for the turnaround project are the same.

- Recommendations are prioritized toward the high impact/high control quadrant of the Recommendation Evaluation Grid.

- A Universal Score Card uniquely designed for each business is a critical measuring tool during the turnaround project through the Reassessing Phase.

- An Advisory Group can help throughout the next four weeks. The group can be a great sounding board for the ideas that are generated during the planning sessions and actual implementation of the plan.

- The business owner's agreement and commitment to the written turnaround plan is critical to the overall success of the project.

CASE I
Miriam's Art and Frame

The assessment is done. Now it is time to determine a turnaround business plan on which your sister-in-law, the business owner, and you can agree. That actually shouldn't be too hard. You analyzed the situation and agreed on what the main problems were. You decided that the business has potential! It is time to get busy, change things that need to be changed and get this business into growth mode.

By the way, the bookkeeper who was taking money is now gone; in fact, she left the very day you discovered the cash shortage problem. This was the first step in the business plan: stop the cash leakage caused by employees.

You believe you have the right people in place and with proper controls and plans, the business should grow over the next few years.

As the accountant, cash management will now be in your control until Miriam's business stabilizes. That should require one or two months.

An Advisory Group may not be needed at first because the first priority is to get cash under control. You don't need an Advisory Group for that. However, the Advisory Group can be helpful when you consider new business models, specifically when it comes to marketing ideas. This Advisory Group could include customers, designers, and Chamber of Commerce members: 3 or 4 people maximum.

The Turnaround Business Plan focuses on controlling cash as the number one priority. Miriam's turnaround business plan looks like this:

MIRIAM'S ART AND FRAME
Turnaround Business Plan

DESCRIPTION OF THE SITUATION

Cash is running out! The office manager has been stealing from the business. Inventory is too large. Cash is used as a draw for many family needs. Children have credit cards paid by Miriam. This cash problem is the most important and top priority problem to address.

Expenses are out of control. The expenses incurred are not in line with the sales. Inventory and Accounts Receivable need to be addressed.

Revenue streams are highly dependent on people who come in the shop. Thus, sales are limited and need to expand. There are many problems that need to be addressed. They are typical of small businesses in trouble. However, cash management is the highest priority.

OPPORTUNITIES AND RISKS

Business seems to be there but there are numerous internal problems that must be addressed. Stabilization of internal operations is a clear focus. From the outside, customers will see few changes. The risk is that Miriam is running out of cash quickly and she may not be able to stay in business past the end of the month without major changes.

BUSINESS MODEL

The business model is simple: Sell art and framing services to the general public at a profit.

TURNAROUND OBJECTIVE

The objective is to stabilize the business first; get cash and expenses under control and then grow the business.

The business will look much the same as it does now but the

internal operations will be much improved. Cash in the bank should be $25,000 to adequately cover ongoing overhead expenses.

MAJOR CHANGES NEEDED TO MAKE NEW BUSINESS MODEL SUCCESSFUL

Framing and art sales are still the major products. However, major changes will be made in the internal workings of the business. More effective cash controls will be developed by the accountant.

An Advisory Group is unnecessary at first. The accountant will handle all internal cash and expense control procedures. An Advisory Group will be invited to share ideas about revenue enhancement. That will be at least three weeks or more into the turnaround process.

OPERATIONS PLAN

All cash disbursements must be approved by the accountant before outlay is made.

All expenses are approved by the accountant or the business owner. Personal spending by children will be eliminated. Collection procedures on past due Accounts Receivable will improve.

Revenue enhancements will be a secondary focus after cash and expenses are in control.

PEOPLE

The right people are currently in place. The office manager was terminated on the very day it was discovered that cash was missing from the bank accounts.

Because Miriam's children are not technically employed by the company, their access to company credit cards will be terminated immediately. Any money they receive should come from Miriam's personal draw.

Miriam's job is managing the front-end of the operations. She will handle sales and supervise production or framing. The back room will be supervised by the accountant.

Business decisions will be made jointly by the owner and the accountant.

UNIVERSAL SCORE CARD DEVELOPMENT

Major measurements of success during the turnaround period should include the following:

Cash in the bank. This can be monitored daily, but for the purpose of this Universal Score Card it will be monitored weekly. The owner and the accountant are the only two allowed to access the cash account.

Accounts Receivable over 90 days. This figure needs to decrease immediately. It is too big for any small business to handle.

Inventory. Inventory must be liquidated to provide cash for the business.

Sales. This figure is important and will become a bigger focus later in the turnaround process.

Total Expenses. This figure needs to be monitored and controlled because of its relationship to cash improvement. Rent is excluded as it obscures the trends.

Current Ratio. This figure should eventually be around the 2.0 mark. Right now, it is monitored for any improvement.

Based on the assessment performed last week, two weeks of data are already loaded on the Universal Score Card. Cash has improved a little but must continue to improve. The Universal Score Card will serve as an excellent gauge of what is going on in the business.

Here is Miriam's Score Card for the first two weeks:

MIRIAM'S ART AND FRAME
TURNAROUND SCORE CARD

Description	Week 1 Assessment	Week 2 Planning	Week 3 Cash	Week 4 Expenses	Week 5 Revenue	Week 6 Reassess	Target
Cash in the bank	2,250	3,972					$25,000
Accounts Receivable over 90 days old	9,250	9,250					1,000
Inventory	12,050	11,130					8,000
Sales	4,980	2,320					8,000
Total Expenses	3,225	1,640					1,800*
Current Ratio	1.0	1.0					1.6

*Excludes Rent

OBSERVATIONS ON RESULTS AFTER WEEK 2

- Business plan is written and in place

- Cash has improved this week because total expenses went down and no new inventory purchased. The focus is on using inventory currently in the warehouse.

- Accounts Receivable will not improve until actual collection work is done. We will immediately begin contacting customers having a balance over 90 days past due and determine how to collect deliquent payments.

CASE II
Knecht Roofing and Construction

It's nice that Kevin has work, now you have to make it profitable work. The assessment showed that our expenses were way out of control. Unfortunately, Kevin needs to stop taking a cash draw for the short term because there is not enough cash to support that habit. That is difficult because, even though his wife works, they have some expensive toys and not having that additional income will hurt. Maybe some of the toys will have to go.

Fortunately there is plenty of work in the market place; Kevin just has to ensure it is profitable work. That might mean fewer but more profitable jobs. Weekly breakeven is 2 jobs and Kevin can't effectively take a draw until they are averaging 3 jobs a week.

The business model is sound in theory. In practice, however, reckless expenses are sabotaging functionality. Accurate accounting information will help here with someone (the accountant) watching and monitoring every expense.

A quick turnaround is critical. Bid history has not reflected adequate gross margin. You, as the Profit Expert, should approve all bids, as Kevin has not been doing that job well. Proper gross margin on each job is vital.

An Advisory Group is not necessary now. The internal operations of the company are the current focus and the accountant can handle that.

KNECHT ROOFING AND CONSTRUCTION
Turnaround Business Plan

DESCRIPTION OF THE SITUATION

Cash is in short supply and Kevin draws $1,000 per week. That cash outlay is problematic as there is not enough cash to pay other expenses. Kevin has some expensive toys that he needs to pay for, thus the need for the weekly draw.

Margins are lower than they should be. The average revenue per job is less than the average expenses per job. Expenses are high.

Major problems to be addressed are low margins and high expenses. Those are the two high priority problems that will be the focus during the first few weeks of the turnaround process.

The opportunities are that the business, with the right controls in place, would be viable. The roofing service is needed in the marketplace and there is plenty of work. The goal is to make the roofing jobs profitable and the business sustainable. Most jobs are currently losing money.

The risk is that with increased prices, the number of jobs won in the bidding process will go down. Still Kevin only needs two jobs per week to breakeven and three jobs per week to make enough profit to support his $1,000 weekly draw.

BUSINESS MODEL

Currently Knecht Roofing does roofing work for contractors building new houses and to a lesser degree, reroofing work and repairs for existing home owners needing that work done. The business makes money when revenue from the roofing jobs exceeds all expenses. That has not happened.

From the outside, the revised business model may not appear much different than it is right now. However, internal structure, processes, and operations will change drastically if Knecht's has any chance of survival.

TURNAROUND OBJECTIVE

The objective is to stabilize the business, concentrating first on expense control, then revenue enhancement. Margins need to increase on all jobs.

MAJOR CHANGES ARE NEEDED TO MAKE THE NEW BUSINESS MODEL SUCCESSFUL

The immediate focus will be on cash control. Kevin, unfortunately, will lose his weekly draw. This is a short-term solution. His draw will return in a few weeks when the cash position improves.

Expenses need to be controlled and decreased immediately. We will evaluate our current supplies to determine if we can decrease costs in any area.

Gross margins on individual jobs must improve. This will occur because of a $500 price increase in the near future.

THE OPERATIONS PLAN

The accountant will manage the cash. All disbursements will be approved by him. Kevin's draw will be eliminated for a few weeks.

Expenses will also be approved by the accountant. The goal is to work on those expenses that can be reduced immediately. Accounts Receivable work will be done reducing the time it takes to collect money from contractors.

Revenue will increase by $500 on all jobs beginning immediately. Some training is involved making Kevin a more profitable bidder on roofing jobs. The number of jobs completed each week must increase to three—all with higher margins than Kevin is currently securing.

PEOPLE

The right people are in place for the turnaround process. The addition of the accountant is influential in controlling cash outlays and expense reduction. Kevin's wife continues as bookkeeper.

An Advisory Group could be used in the future, but is currently unnecessary. This Advisory Group will focus on marketing as the accountant will contribute all necessary internal operations expertise.

Kevin will be the main contact on the jobs. He will ensure the jobs are effectively completed on time and under budget. He will add people as jobs increase.

UNIVERSAL SCORE CARD

The Score Card focuses on expense control and gross margins for each job. There are two weeks of data already compiled on the Score Card. Those critical indicators include the following:

Cash in the bank. This indicator is key to business success—especially when Kevin's weekly draw is involved.

Accounts Receivable. This number must to be reduced. Normally, contractors pay within three or four weeks. Retail consumers should pay in cash when the reroofing jobs are completed. The target is to have no more than two job's worth of account receivables at any one time—at least for now.

Revenue per job. This is also a key indicator. The target is $4,000 per job where currently the average job is $3,400. This $4,000 per job, will give us adequate gross margin to be profitable (with three jobs per week).

Costs per job. This indicator will help us track expenses on each individual job. This needs to improve.

Jobs per week. Two jobs per week will not cut it. Three jobs per week are needed so that Kevin can take a weekly draw.

Income per week. This indicator quickly shows what the total week's picture looks like. If we concentrate the profitability of each job, then the week is profitable as well.

Current Ratio. This ratio helps the accountant better understand the business's cash and current assets position. A normal current ratio would be around 2.0. In this case the target current ratio is 0.5, which is not good, but is certainly better than what it is now.

The Score Card below indicates Knecht's first two weeks of data in the turnaround process. The key indicators were determined during the assessment period.

KNECHT ROOFING AND CONSTRUCTION
TURNAROUND SCORE CARD

Description	Week 1 Assessment	Week 2 Planning	Week 3 Cash	Week 4 Expenses	Week 5 Revenue	Week 6 Reassess	Target
Cash in the bank	1,250	2,200					$10,000
Accounts Receivable	15,120	16,120					7,500
Revenue per job	3,495	3,400					4,000
Costs and Expenses per job	3,589	4,050					3,000
Jobs Completed	1	1					3
Net Income	(940)	(650)					3,000
Current Ratio	.3	.3					.5

OBSERVATIONS ON RESULTS AFTER WEEK 2

• Turnaround Business Plan is written, approved and implemented.

• Cash has improved because Kevin completed a reroofing job this week and was paid at the end of the job.

• Week 2 does not paint a rosy picture but with new controls in place, indicators should improve over the next few weeks.

• Collection work has started and should show results next week. Accounts Receivable must decrease by over 50%.

• Kevin must consider strategies that will reduce personal spending until his draws resume.

CASE III
Sherwood's SureSave Market and Auto Repair

The operational assessment found that Sherwood's has a great business location; the concern is getting the right business there. They have the right people, at least for the auto repair shop. And you are the right person to work with them as an accountant and business advisor.

Cash in the bank is decreasing so the need to do something different is paramount. Gas sales are also quickly decreasing and the convenience store seems doomed. The business plan will focus on keeping tight control on expenses until the revenue situation turns around.

The major concern is in developing and marketing a new business model. An Advisory Group might be very beneficial in brainstorming ideas about a new business model.

This advisory group could include Chamber of Commerce members, SCORE (Service Core of Retired Executives) volunteers, Small Business Development Center consultants, and even the manager of the new grocery store across the street. Their job is to generate revenue-generating ideas for this location.

SHERWOOD'S SURESAVE AND AUTO REPAIR
Turnaround Business Plan

DESCRIPTION OF THE SITUATION

Sherwood's SureSave and Auto Repair is in a great location for car-related businesses. The auto repair business has always provided great margins that enable comfortable living for the father and son who run the auto repair shop. The convenience store always held its own profit-wise until the supermarket opened across the street.

Now the convenience store volume is plummeting along with gasoline sales (about 10% a week). Auto repair work is holding its own. But, the big draw of gasoline is no longer there. Increased revenue generation is the central issue to be addressed.

Major problem areas addressed focus on marketing-related activities. New products and services need to be developed to replace convenience store revenue. This focus will be on something that is auto related. This could be traditional products and service such as tires and tune-ups or body work. Or it could focus on electronics: audio systems for all types of motor vehicles, from cars to motor homes to possibly boats. The electronics idea is very intriguing.

The opportunities here are great. They have a great location and a chance for revenue growth with products and services that complement the auto repair business. The convenience store needed major remodeling and the gasoline tanks are old and need to be replaced soon. Investment of some sort is necessary and this is the opportunity to get into something that might not have the same environmental impact as gasoline and cigarettes.

The risks are that the Sherwoods will make the wrong decisions about what to do with their business property. This could force them into a lower standard-of-living or possibly putting the property and business up for sale.

BUSINESS MODEL

The previous business model was to entice customers to drive their vehicles onto the property to spend money in some way—either at the convenience store or auto repair bays. This model has worked for many years, but because of new competition across the street, it will not work in the future and must quickly change.

Internal controls are not a problem. Management is good; marketing and revenue generation will change dramatically. The business will stay alive and prosper with new products and services which will be tested in the coming weeks.

TURNAROUND OBJECTIVE

The objective is to stabilize the business first, replace revenue lost as a result of a new supermarket across the street and then, grow the business.

THE OPERATIONS PLAN

The Operations Plan focuses on the expertise of the people involved in the business. The Sherwoods will maintain total control of the auto repair business. The accountant will run feasibility studies on new products and services for the convenience store location. The accountant will also institute an Advisory Group for help in considering new marketing ideas.

Marketing ideas are considered from all four quadrants in the geometric marketing model. (See Chapter Seven — Increasing Revenue, page 161.) Sherwood's list of loyal customers is long, so developing new products and services for existing customers is at the forefront of ideas considered.

Cash and expenses, in general, have not been a problem in the past. However, continued vigilance is needed to ensure that cash and expense items remain tightly controlled until the enhanced business model is implemented.

PEOPLE

The right people are in place doing the work through the turn-around period—especially the Sherwoods. The three workers in the convenience store might turn over because of their potential lack of experience in future products and services.

The Advisory Group is critical to the success of this business turn-around. This group could be made up of people, possibly local store owners, who are great at marketing their own products and services. The new supermarket manager from across the street may be an ideal member of the Advisory Group. If the new products and services are designed well, he may be able to promote them through his own store. Other possible members of the Advisory Group include a loyal customer and an auto parts supplier.

As mentioned, the Sherwoods will focus on the auto repair bays and the accountant will focus on what to do with the space currently filled with the convenience store that will soon be empty. The accountant will chair the Advisory Group and offer marketing advice from a numbers perspective. He will also monitor the business numbers, including tests on new products and services.

THE UNIVERSAL SCORE CARD

The Universal Score Card focuses on those indicators that need to improve so the business can thrive once again. The Score Card will focus on cash management and expense control. There are two weeks of data already compiled on the Score Card below. Enhanced revenue generation is the key to turnaround success. Those critical indicators include the following:

Cash in the bank. This indicator is key to business success.

Sales—Auto Shop. This part of the business must remain stable and growing to sustain any new business venture until it gets going again.

Sales—Gas and Convenience Store. Sales from the convenience store and gasoline will probably not last through the turnaround phase of the business. Sales have been dropping by 10% a week.

Total Costs and Expenses. This indicator will help us keep expenses in line during the transition phase. Good management here is critical because total revenue will be down while the convenience store is remodeled.

Current Ratio. This ratio helps the accountant better understand the cash and current assets position in the business. A normal current ratio would be in the area of 2.0. In this case, the target current ratio is 1.5 which is good and somewhat better than the current indicator.

Sherwood's Score Card looks like this at the end of the second week.

SHERWOOD'S SURESAVE
TURNAROUND SCORE CARD

Description	Week 1 Assessment	Week 2 Planning	Week 3 Cash	Week 4 Expenses	Week 5 Revenue	Week 6 Reassess	Target
Cash	40,602	38,996					$50,000
Sales – Auto Shop and New Audio	7,750	8,100					35,000
Sales Gas and Convenience Store	10,285	9,125					0
Total Costs and Expenses	18,200	23,073					10,000
Current Ratio	1.3	1.3					1.5

OBSERVATIONS ON RESULTS AFTER WEEK 2

- Targets are established and two weeks of data are entered into the Score Card.

- Cash is stable, but lower, because mortgage payments are due this week.

- The Advisory Group is formed and meet for the first time. Their main task is to generate marketing ideas for the convenience store location.

- You have evaluated payroll expenses closely. They appear to be higher so you will monitor them closely.

- You will evaluate every idea for producing revenue at this location.

FIVE

STEP 3
Improving Cash Management

The initial assessment is done; the Turnaround Business Plan is written. Recommendations and action steps are outlined and prioritized using the Recommendation Evaluation Grid. Now, it is time to convert recommendations into action.

The Universal Turnaround Model below illustrates where you currently are in the turnaround process. This is the third step. The purpose of Step 3 is to implement the part of the business plan developed for improving cash management.

The outside ring helps us understand where you are in the turnaround process. The resources in the

UNIVERSAL TURNAROUND MODEL

middle of the model are also important, especially the accounting information.

WHY CASH FIRST?

Cash is a *right now* issue. This is where you must *stop the bleeding,* so to speak, because cash is a precious commodity and must be used effectively. Gaining control of cash is the first major implementation step after business plans are completed. Why? Because cash is an internal system, especially outgoing cash, that is controlled more easily than expenses or revenue generation.

Shortage of cash is where most business owners first realize they have problems. There could be enough cash in the bank right now to make it through the next month or two. That does not mean, however, that the business is in a good cash position.

From the accounting information, you should be able to find out exactly how much cash there is, or should be, in the bank account. Those two numbers should be the same or easily reconcilable.

The resources in the center of the Universal Turnaround Model are critically important in this step. The accounting information, when up-to-date, provides much needed data about the business's cash needs. Look at how much cash is coming into and going out of the business as well as when checks are written. This accounting information can then be reconciled with the bank information (now available on the internet) to ensure the cash records correlate.

Industry data can also indicate how businesses in your industry are performing. This information is usually in a percentage or ratio format. This is not something that is examined every day, but probably once a month would suffice to see how your business compares to similar businesses.

The Advisory Group can offer counsel about what has worked for them in the past as they have dealt with cash issues. This information might be the most important of the three recommended resources.

OBJECTIVES

Just *receiving* more cash is different than *improving* cash management. Cash management is the active involvement in managing the working capital or the *cash inflow*. You want to increase that amount and accelerate transfers from the bank accounts of those who owe you money into your own bank accounts. Cash management is also the active involvement of managing the *cash outflow*. You want to decrease that amount and decelerate transfers of cash from your bank accounts into accounts where you owe money.

The major objective of this step is to implement a solid cash management system. That means that you know how much cash is coming into the business and when it is coming in. It also means that you implement a plan for payments, determining the best method for cash to leave the business. More is required than merely putting revenue into the bank when received and writing checks when you decide to pay vendors and employees.

CASH CONTROL

As the small business accountant, this is an area that you want to retain partial or complete control. Perhaps the business is going through cash too quickly or making unnecessary expenditures. An objective voice in the process could bring cash control into perspective for the business owner.

Cash control and expense control work together. Both areas are centered within the business and can be brought under control quickly. By that I don't mean that all your cash problems will go away quickly. What I do mean is that you can have an almost immediate influence on how cash goes out of the business.

Cash management systems were evaluated during the assessment step. Now it is time to take action. The current status of the business's cash accounts should be obtainable by looking at the available accounting information and bank account records. Here are some other suggestions:

Take control of the cash accounts. No cash leaves the company without your approval. Cash going out is easier to control than cash coming in. Many times sales cannot be predicted effectively, so that incoming cash is harder to predict and plan for. Outgoing cash is easier to predict, especially in the short term.

Determine how much cash it takes to run the business for a month. This includes the next payroll period and all the payments made to suppliers and contractors. This will prepare you with adequate cash when needed.

Monitor cash on a daily, weekly and monthly basis. And who has the responsibility to watch the cash accounts? You, as the small business accountant, are the best person for the job.

Of course it is difficult to get "blood out of the proverbial turnip." But there are ways to manage cash more effectively—both cash inflow and outflow

DECREASE CASH OUTFLOWS

Let's focus on ways to decrease the amount and flow of cash leaving the business.

Here are the questions that need to be addressed today: Where is the cash going? What can I do in the next 24 hours to change the outflow of cash?

Here are some ways to reduce cash outflows:

- Approve all expenditures yourself (or the business owner).

- Freeze spending on anything that is not critical.

- Lengthen payables. If you are on good terms with your vendors, it may be possible to lengthen the terms of those payments from 30 to 60, or perhaps even 90 days. If cash is the real problem, this would allow you to keep more cash in the business for a longer period of time.

This has a short-term effect in increasing cash because in 60 or 90 days, you will still be making monthly payments to these vendors. However if cash is needed quickly, here is one alternative: Immediately seek to lengthen those agreements by at least 30 days. Your vendors might not be terribly happy with you. But, business survival is more important than their happiness.

- Look for suppliers, which have either lower prices or better payment terms. This strategy can work particularly well when you have been current on your payments for a year or more.

- Decrease rent if possible. Again, this is hard to do in the short term. But, over a longer period of time, it might be a viable option.

- Decrease payroll. Perhaps this is a last resort. But, it is something that will have an immediate effect on cash.

- Freeze personal draws as a last resort to preserve cash.

In other words, do what can be done to stabilize cash—today. Cancel company credit cards for anyone who does not need one. Stop the free lunches.

If the business currently has bad credit, there's probably not much that can be done to correct the situation. Once things are turned around in a month or so, definite steps can be taken to improve the credit through the judicious use of cash.

These ideas tie together closely with the expense reduction part of the turnaround process, which will be discussed in the next chapter.

Now let's switch to the second objective: What can you do to manage the cash coming into the business?

INCREASE CASH INFLOWS

Here are some ways to increase the amount and flow of cash coming into the business. These issues should have been answered during the assessment phase of the turnaround process. Here are some recommendations for quick action:

- Emphasize cash generators in the business. Some products and services are more profitable than others; promote them.

- Promote cash sales instead of credit sales. Take sales anyway they come but cash is better than credit.

- Limit credit terms encouraging customers to purchase with cash yet not to the extent that sales decrease.

The goal is to develop ways to convert sales and assets (like Accounts Receivable) into cash. Here are some additional ideas:

- Tell customers who owe you money that if they pay today, you will gladly give them a bigger discount—five to ten percent should be enough.

- Ask the owner to contact customers and say, "My accountant is on my back to get this paid. Will you help me by paying this off?"

- Unload inventory more quickly. What types of sales incentives can you use right now to increase the sale of existing inventory?

- Factor business receivables (selling your receivables to another business). Sometimes the interest rate can get down to 2 or 3 %. This is a very expensive option.

In some cases, cash problems are seasonal in nature. These problems can be handled differently, perhaps using a line of credit to augment cash positions during certain times of the year.

ADDITIONAL SOURCES OF CASH

In some cases, particularly in small and growing businesses, the business model is not strong enough to create enough cash to handle the outflow. Additional sources of cash may be necessary if you sense that business growth warrants additional capital.

- Additional sources of debt or equity capital. This might be a loan on the family home or a loan from a relative.

- Selling equipment to a leasing company and leasing it back can raise cash in the business.

- Transfer of cash into the business from the business owner's other personal assets. This might include a second mortgage on the owner's house, use of personal credit cards to pay company expenses, or possibly selling personal assets to generate cash. Some assets can be converted to cash quickly, some not.

- Other Investors. These people might be friends and family members who believe in what you are doing. It could be a vendor or other type of supplier, or even a customer who wants to help you through this tough spot with either investment capital (for part ownership in the company) or a loan of some sort. Loans will probably be easier to obtain and quicker than additional equity capital, especially if you have some sort of collateral (outside the business) to back your loan request.

As the company's accountant and trusted advisor, perhaps you would be willing to invest in the business through cash, services rendered in lieu of cash or some other investment. This should have been decided in the written agreement described in Chapter Two.

- Angel Investors. Angel capital is cash that comes from an investor based on idea alone or early development work on a company's new product or idea. These investors want to get their money back with sometimes very large returns within a year or so. They will take an ownership interest in the company, wanting to be bought out when additional funding or investment capital is needed in a year or two.

  This source may be viable in the short term if your product or service is exceptionally well-received, but underfunded. Still, thirty days is a very quick turnaround for getting cash into the business.

There are other sources of cash but these are the main ones. Perhaps family members of the business owner would put money into the business expecting little return. Your future inheritance might be much smaller but it could provide needed cash now.

I have encountered another interesting issue in my practice. Some business owners have ample cash at the present, but fear it will soon dry up. If this is the case, the biggest problem today is not cash per se, but rather expense control. That will be covered in the next chapter.

Improving the cash management system within your business should be a high priority irrespective of the business's condition. But, it is the number one priority to be addressed if you will turn the business around in four weeks.

Frequently Asked Questions

How do you know that more cash should be infused into the business?

You know the business needs more cash when there is not enough to cover the next week's planned cash outflows. If your assessment reveals the business model will work with some changes, then that might be evidence enough to invest more cash into the business.

If your assessment indicated that the business model will not work, even with changes, don't invest one more dime. Liquidate! Transfer all assets into a cash position.

Can vendors help you get into a better cash position?

Yes. Be open in paying vendors what you can and ask for special assistance right now. Tell them about the problems. They may recommend some options that will improve business.

Big suppliers or big businesses have special programs for small businesses so that they are paid quickly when invoices are received.

Should money from others be considered an investment or a loan?

It depends. What do the people bring with them besides their money? If an investor brings talents, then he can get or give equity dollars. Can you repay the loan from foreseeable cash flow? Both options are viable and can be implemented quickly, if necessary, and the right situation presents itself.

What about venture capitalists?

Venture capitalists are people or companies who invest in small and growing companies with the intention to cash out later with a large profit. A venture capitalist will take an ownership interest in the company, perhaps even a large or majority ownership interest.

Dealing with venture capitalists is a long-term solution. It is not likely that they will hand you a check this week to meet your needs. Most venture capitalists have specified processes to follow to secure an appointment with them. So this option will probably not solve immediate cash needs.

What about going public with a stock offering?

This might not be a bad idea if you have confidence in the revised business plan. It is more long-range in nature. It takes time to prepare all the things that need to be accomplished before going public. Our focus here is on a thirty-day turnaround which would preclude our going public for more cash.

SUMMARY—WHERE YOU SHOULD BE AT THIS POINT

Cash management is the focus during this step. At the end of Step 3, recommendations should be implemented with high impact over which you have high control for improving cash management. As the Profit Expert, you control, with the owner's permission, all cash disbursements.

You have implemented appropriate business model changes to increase cash flow into the business. These changes may not be apparent to customers as they are mostly internal in nature.

Control mechanisms are created so that cash is easily monitored by you and the business owner. All unnecessary and secondary payments are stopped immediately to conserve cash.

All sources of cash have been evaluated, including further investment by the owner or possibly another investor. You have also considered securing additional capital through loans or venture capitalists.

You and the business owner are aware of exactly how much cash is needed to run the business on a weekly and monthly basis into the next quarter. You approve every check leaving the business on a daily basis to know where cash is going. You have stopped all unnecessary payments to conserve cash.

This first step is internal. As a Profit Expert, you can make a quick and important impact on controlling cash management. Five days or one week is allocated for this step.

Although this is the third week of the turnaround project and controlling cash is the major focus, cash control systems should be established in the near future to help monitor cash on a daily and weekly basis.

CHAPTER FIVE
IMPROVING CASH MANAGEMENT
Key Learning Points

- The shortage of cash is where most business owners first realize they have problems.

- Profit Experts have natural expertise in controlling cash. You know what type of controls are appropriate for this particular client. Accounting information is critical right now for the proper monitoring of cash.

- Controlling cash is the first actual implementation step of the six steps in the Universal Turnaround Model. It is the first step because the business is bleeding cash and you have a significant impact on controlling cash flow.

- All sources of cash have advantages and disadvantages. In the short-term, the business must depend on better cash management to solve cash flow problems.

CASE I
Miriam's Art and Frame

Cash flow is the major problem at Miriam's Art and Frame. Of course the bookkeeper was fired as soon as it was discovered that she was pilfering from the business.

You see a great improvement in the cash position. Here are other specific action steps taken during the first week of Miriam's turnaround project:

Cash was monitored on a daily basis and all cash outlays are approved by Miriam or you. She stopped giving money to her kids. Although this was a personal draw situation, she needed the cash in her business to stop the bleeding.

Miriam stopped feeding cash to other businesses and charities from the cash account. The credit cards used by her children were cancelled.

When possible, vendor payments were delayed to 60-day terms.

As many purchases as possible were made by credit card to conserve cash.

Much was accomplished on Accounts Receivables to collect funds that were due for more than 90 days. In some cases, one phone call did the trick. In other situations, you simply had to furnish a copy of the invoice because the original had been misplaced or lost.

Here is Miriam's Score Card for the week:

MIRIAM'S ART AND FRAME
TURNAROUND SCORE CARD

Description	Week 1 Assessment	Week 2 Planning	Week 3 Cash	Week 4 Expenses	Week 5 Revenue	Week 6 Reassess	Target
Cash in the bank	2,250	3,972	8,707				$25,000
Accounts Receivable over 90 days old	9,250	9,250	8,100				1,000
Inventory	12,050	11,130	9,030				8,000
Sales	4,980	2,320	5,625				8,000
Total Expenses	3,225	1,640	1,890				1,800*
Current Ratio	1.0	1.0	1.0				1.6

*Excludes Rent

OBSERVATIONS ON RESULTS AFTER WEEK 3

- The cash position improved dramatically during this week. This was because of time spent collecting overdue Accounts Receivable, reducing inventory and generating more cash sales.

- Accounting information is critical in analyzing what is happening inside the business.

- Inventory adjustments are not easy but can be done having direct effect on cash.

CASE II
Knecht Roofing and Construction

Cash flow is a major problem mainly because of insufficient margins. Kevin has no idea why he has no cash in the bank. He often brags about winning every bid so he feels he can get plenty of work. Cash accounts reflect the correlation between what he is charging per job and the corresponding costs per job. These indicators are monitored closely.

All cash leaving the bank account needs approval with checks counter-signed by you.

Accounts Receivable is monitored closely. Contractors should pay within two weeks and consumers should pay upon job completion.

Bid prices were raised $500 (about 15%) per job. Kevin might win fewer jobs but the jobs won are profitable. Each job must be profitable

The $1,000 draw stops until Kevin gets three jobs a week. And while this does cramp his style a bit, it is a necessary step right now.

Although this is the week to focus on cash management, you will need to discuss marketing in the upcoming weeks. Now is the time to start thinking about this. Perhaps you could begin establishing the Advisory Group.

Here is Kevin Knecht's Score Card for the week:

KNECHT ROOFING AND CONSTRUCTION
TURNAROUND SCORE CARD

Description	Week 1 Assessment	Week 2 Planning	Week 3 Cash	Week 4 Expenses	Week 5 Revenue	Week 6 Reassess	Target
Cash in the bank	1,250	2,200	2,950				$10,000
Accounts Receivable	15,120	16,120	19,620				7,500
Revenue per job	3,495	3,400	3,550				4,000
Costs and Expenses per job	3,589	4,050	2,925				3,000
Jobs Completed	1	1	2				3
Net Income	(940)	(650)	1,250				3,000
Current Ratio	.3	.3	.3				.5

OBSERVATIONS ON RESULTS AFTER WEEK 3

- Net income is up $1,900 over the previous week. This is a result of more profitable bidding and better expense control.

- Accounts Receivable is up because one of the two jobs completed this week was for a contractor and on credit.

- Revenue per job is up because of better bidding.

CASE III
Sherwood's SureSave Market and Auto Repair

Cash is important, but right now there is sufficient cash in the bank. Family member employees are notified of the importance of keeping enough cash on hand until revenue turns around.

Any new products will be tested. Cash must be preserved for investment in new revenue-generating ventures for the convenience store portion of the business.

Expenses are under control for now—payroll might go down in the convenience store as you shorten the hours. No new purchases have been made for convenience store inventory. Other significant work has been done during the week to control expenses.

The Advisory Group met for the first time. Members include the grocery store manager from across the street, Tom Sherwood, the father, a consultant from the Small Business Development Center, a marketing professor from a nearby private college and you, the accountant. You are the chairperson of the Advisory Group.

The Advisory Group began brainstorming on what to do with the convenience store portion of the location. The group did decide that selling automotive electronic systems, beginning with audio systems, might be the best complement to auto repair work. It is worth a try, even though the revenue-building step is two weeks away.

Tom's son, Scott, is key to the transition as he has installed a number of audio systems for past customers.

The Advisory Group suggested that audio systems could be tested by running special promotions for two weeks. If the test is successful, then the convenience store could be remodeled into a showroom for various electronics products. The grocery store manager was willing to pass out fliers to his customers.

Here is the Score Card for Sherwood's for week 3.

SHERWOOD'S SURESAVE
TURNAROUND SCORE CARD

Description	Week 1 Assessment	Week 2 Planning	Week 3 Cash	Week 4 Expenses	Week 5 Revenue	Week 6 Reassess	Target
Cash	40,602	38,996	47,073				$50,000
Sales – Auto Shop and New Audio	7,750	8,100	7,900				35,000
Sales Gas and Convenience Store	10,285	9,125	7,937				0
Total Costs and Expenses	18,200	23,073	16,733				10,000
Current Ratio	1.3	1.3	1.3				1.5

OBSERVATIONS ON RESULTS AFTER WEEK 3

- Significant cash improvements were made this week even though sales in the convenience store continued to drop. No additional inventory purchases were made for the convenience store.

- Auto repair sales remained steady. Most sales are collected when the work is completed. Sherwood's has very few credit accounts in the auto repair bays. This leads to cash account additions every day.

- Net expenses were down $6,000. That would have gone down $11,000 without a depreciation entry. Expense disbursements were low during the week because no major bills were due.

- No payroll was due this week.

SIX

STEP 4
Reducing Expenses

This is the fourth week of the turnaround process and the focus turns to reducing expenses. A Turnaround Business Plan was created with attention to changes and improvements that could be made quickly—for example, 30 days or less. The first step was getting control of the cash account. No cash leaves the bank without the owner's approval or, if appropriate, your approval. Although it is closely related to controlling cash, reducing expenses is not the same. Cash is easier to control in the short run; that is why it is the first step.

The **Universal Turnaround Model** (right) illustrates exactly where you are in the turnaround process. This is the fourth of six steps. You are moving quickly out of necessity. But you're not moving haphazardly; you are moving with preciseness.

UNIVERSAL TURNAROUND MODEL

MONITORING AND REASSESSING

ASSESSING THE SITUATION

ACCOUNTING INFORMATION
—
ADVISORY GROUP
—
INDUSTRY DATA

INCREASING REVENUE

PLANNING THE TURNAROUND

REDUCING EXPENSES

IMPROVING CASH MANAGEMENT

CASH MANAGEMENT FIRST; EXPENSE REDUCTION SECOND

Cash is where you have the most control; cash management is the first emphasis. The assumption is not that the cash situation is positive, but you have better control over the cash flow, especially cash that is leaving the account. This is the result of work performed in the previous step.

After cash management, expense management is where you have the most control. It is also internally-based. Expenses are incurred on a daily basis but the corresponding cash to pay expenses might not leave the cash account until later. Thus, the bank might be flush with cash, but in reality, all cash is committed to pay expenses already incurred.

Employees have the most influence on expense control. Businesses have greater control over expenses than in increasing revenue in that expenses can be adjusted today whereas revenue can take much longer to impact.

It doesn't matter whether your business is in crisis or not, you should always be looking for ways to reduce expenses. All employees must be engaged in reducing waste. Every employee usually has ideas where expenses could be lowered.

Specific definitions are helpful. Businesses incur two types of expenses. Usually expenses are explained as a percentage of sales. They should be in line with other businesses of your industry.

Variable Expenses: These expenses vary according to sales. As sales go up, so do these expenses. If sales go to zero, then variable expenses drop to zero. They are entirely related to production or sales. Examples include raw materials, sales commissions, travel-related sales expenses, etc.

Fixed Expenses: These expenses are not related to actual sales but are incurred by the business every month. Examples of fixed expenses include advertising, leases for equipment, vehicles, etc.

The objective is to reduce expenses as much as possible with minimal effect on sales and still have the business run effectively. This objective must be in place irrespective of whether or not the business is in a crisis turnaround situation.

The important question here is where to look for expenses that can be reduced. What is the breakeven for the business? The breakeven analysis was introduced in the Assessment chapter and is re-created below. The purpose of the breakeven analysis is to determine what amount of sales is necessary to cover all expenses.

That is an important number to know. It will allow you to determine how much needs to be cut from the expense category in order to meet the breakeven target. It is not likely, but possible, that the business is out of control on the expense side of the income statement. There may not be enough sales coming in to cover all the expenses. In that case, this step is the most important in the turnaround process. However, in most cases, there are problems on both the sales and the expenses side.

Here is the sample breakeven analysis (in this case for a month):

Formula	Sales	$ 50,000
Minus	Variable Costs	$ 20,000
Equals	Gross Profit Margin	$ 30,000
Divided by	Units Sold	3,000
Equals	Gross Profit Margin per Unit	$ 10
	Fixed Costs	$ 15,000
Divided by	Gross Profit Margin per Unit	$ 10
Equals	Breakeven Units	1,500

This breakeven analysis quickly demonstrates to everyone in the organization what needs to be done financially in order to be profitable each week, or at least be self-sustaining. Expense reduction is as important as revenue generation in making the breakeven analysis look better. Both variable and fixed expenses need to be evaluated and action steps taken, where appropriate, to reduce expenses.

WORK PROCESS ANALYSIS

Another major question has to do with work processes. Three major activities exist within every small business—Production, Accounting, and Marketing. Each has independent and collective work processes. Each is trying to meet the needs and expectations of internal and external customers.

Each of these major activities has key work processes that are analyzed closely for possible expense reductions. Expense control makes you observe work processes more objectively. Now, the focus is on how to provide the same service or manufacture the same product faster, cheaper and better.

The major work processes were outlined and evaluated during the assessment phase of the turnaround project. A work process, described earlier, is the way work gets completed within the business. Hopefully, work processes are replicable and standardized. There may be two, or fifteen, major work processes.

Work processes are prime candidates for expense reduction both in the variable and fixed categories. Imagine the impact on expense reduction if one, two or three work processes are eliminated or combined.

Each of the different processes needs to be analyzed to ascertain if expense reduction is possible. The following questions will help you perform a simple work process analysis:

What does the customer (internal and external) want at the end of the process?

What are the steps in the work process that must to be completed in order to ensure that the customer is satisfied at the end of the process?

What unnecessary steps in the process could be eliminated?

What would you suggest to improve the process?

Where can you reduce expenses immediately?

Together, with the owner, determine which expenses have a high impact on the business and are easily controlled. The Recommendation Evaluation Grid was introduced in the Chapter Four and the format concept is used again to evaluate expense reduction.

It is similar to the exercise presented in the Planning chapter. When recommendations were evaluated, the Recommendation Evaluation Grid was used to prioritize them. Now, the focus is exclusively on expense reduction so the grid changes a little.

This demonstrates one process of evaluating expenses. And as you evaluate individual expenses you should consider two major questions:

1. *How much impact does this particular expense have on the profitability of the business?*
2. *And how much control do you have over that particular expense?*

Control is the central issue. What are the monthly expenses that could be reduced immediately? That is where quadrant analysis can be helpful. You can use a four-quadrant table for many types of analysis. It is used three times in this book. The technique is very effective in putting order into your thinking process.

The table has four quadrants and is used to sort various expenses by control and impact. You are searching for expenses that have a high impact on the business over which you have high control—those expenses are displayed in quadrant 1. Together, you and the business owner can sort expenses, or you can sort them alone and then present them to the business owner.

RECOMMENDATION EVALUATION GRID

	High Control	Low Control
High Impact	1	2
Low Impact	3	4

During the Assessment phase of the turnaround project, strengths, weaknesses, opportunities and threats were evaluated. Certain recommendations for necessary changes were developed at the end of that phase. Many times more recommendations are made than can be adequately implemented during the 30-day turnaround period. The evaluation grid enables you to sort those change recommendations into priority order.

Three useful tools in analyzing expenses have been discussed so far:

- **Breakeven Analysis.** This tool determines what sales level is necessary to cover all expenses currently incurred.

- **Work Process Analysis.** This tool enables you to analyze the work processes in the business's three major functions—Marketing, Accounting, and Production. This analysis focuses on customer needs and is a good way to determine how resources can be used more effectively.

- **Recommendation Evaluation Grid.** This tool enables you to distinguish those expenses which have a high impact on the business and over which you have high control.

These three are very effective in looking for expenses that can be lowered or eliminated.

I am frequently asked questions about expense reduction within certain businesses. Those questions and the corresponding answers are summarized below:

Frequently Asked Questions

How do I identify expenses that should be cut?

Some expenses go up and down on a monthly basis. These are expenses that could possibly be eliminated or reduced dramatically. Eliminate expenses that don't contribute to sales as much as they cost. Experiment by eliminating some expenses for 30 days to see what happens.

How can I reduce advertising costs without reducing sales?

Advertising is an expense that is controllable. It is important to track which advertising approaches work and which do not. Then, eliminate those that do not. Or eliminate advertising expenses that have the least impact on revenue.

Which advertising is bringing in the most sales? The least? Eliminate the least and expand the best. Response can be quick.

What if payroll is the largest expense? How can it be cut?

In most cases, payroll is the largest expense. Some general rules apply: If you must lay people off or downsize the organization, choose people who have the least impact on revenue generation.

Consider voluntary programs first. Also, you may have an employee who shares your vision for recovery and is able to work for free, understanding that there will be a payoff in the near future. I know of one employee who worked for free for an entire year.

Is it all right to cut someone's paycheck?

Yes, but the owner must be willing to take a cut as well. It is easier to require a cut across-the-board than target certain employees' paychecks. It may be easier to cut benefits than pay.

If you must lay off employees, what is the general rule for paying severance?

For severance pay, the general rule is one week's pay for each year worked. This is true when you don't intend to replace that position immediately. If someone is fired for just cause, then generally no severance pay is awarded.

Also, many small businesses don't award severance pay because they cannot afford it. In a turnaround situation where you have 30 days to make a significant impact, severance pay is generally not a viable option.

What if the owner doesn't want to cut a particular expense?

He may have a pet project or something that he just doesn't want to give up. It could be a car or a flashy, unnecessary piece of equipment. Talk about the impact of those particular expenses and offer alternatives.

This could be a downsizing decision that is necessary but is extremely difficult for the owner because it will impact people who have been with the business from the beginning. Perhaps they have been extremely loyal to the owner and have not taken paychecks at times. Now things have changed and downsizing is inevitable.

How do I negotiate a reduction in rent or interest?

Vendors, like everyone else, may have a stronger commitment to your small business than you realize. Most vendors will forgive the interest portion of a payment if you promise to pay by a certain time.

Rent abatements are possible for certain times if you promise to pay on a future date. Replacing a tenant is expensive and time-consuming. A reasonable landlord will often make concessions to avoid that process.

What about bartering services for other services? Is it legal?

Yes, bartering is legal and done frequently between small businesses. The accounting is tricky but possible. Your client may approach each vendor to see if they may consider a trade in lieu of payment.

Should I cancel insurance to save money?

Probably not. The risk in terminating insurance coverage completely is generally too great, even if it the expense is considerable. However, you may want to re-evaluate current coverage.

What tasks and processes could be replaced by automation?

Most automation in small business comes in the form of computerization. A receptionist might be eliminated in favor of an automated answering system.

What idle equipment could be put to use or discarded?

Take inventory of all business equipment. See what is used ineffectively. Sell it to another business or, if you could still use it, consider selling it to a leasing company and then lease it back.

SUMMARY—WHERE YOU SHOULD BE AT THIS POINT

The focus in this step has been on expense reduction and control. Every expense category of the income statement (and hopefully there is an income statement) has been analyzed and discussed with the owner. Employees helped brainstorm expense reduction. Action steps are taken to reduce expenses.

The expense reduction step is completed, and an expense control system is implemented which includes active monitoring of expenses and analysis of how those expenses can be minimized on a permanent basis.

The Advisory Group was consulted on expense reduction strategy and tactics. Their experience could easily provide other options on controlling expenses more effectively or eliminating them altogether.

This is a one-week phase of the turnaround project. Not all expense reductions have been completed this week but they have begun. Don't give up on the process. It will take longer to see the results of some expense reductions, but they will come.

CHAPTER SIX
REDUCING EXPENSES

Key Learning Points

- A Profit Expert is highly influential in expense reduction. Following cash management, expense reduction should be your next focus. Every major expense category should be analyzed to ensure that it is at its most effective level. Don't let someone else do the analysis; it's your job.

- Expense categories with high impact and where you also have high control should receive the highest priority. Not all expense reductions can be completed in a week but they can be started.

- Critical expenses should show up on the Score Card that was developed in the project's planning phase. They are then monitored on a regular, perhaps daily, weekly, or monthly, basis.

- Expense control and sales generation should work together. The intention is to cut expenses that have the least impact on sales generation.

- Plans are implemented that have almost an immediate effect on the business's expense level. This should include a breakeven analysis as well as an evaluation of both variable and fixed expenses.

- Employees may provide useful expense-reduction ideas.

CASE I
Miriam's Art and Frame Shop

Based on the analysis of the different expense categories, steps were taken to control cash more effectively and to reduce expenses. Each expense category has been evaluated. Action steps have been prioritized in the high control, high impact expense areas. Now it is time to examine all expenses. It is also time to cut all unnecessary costs.

Different ideas are considered: Should the production workers be paid on a piece-meal basis? Should the shop move to a lower-rent district? (She is currently on a month-to-month lease.) Should she have a fire sale to eliminate old framing inventory and art pieces that have been around too long? What is the payroll? All expenses are subject to scrutiny.

Inventory is decreasing to a manageable level. Smaller inventory means less storage space and possibly less space needed overall. Accounts Receivable is decreasing. Reduction in both Inventory and Accounts Receivable result in a better cash position.

One employee fell short of expectations and was terminated. The remaining employees are contributors to the profit line. All credit cards for family members were cancelled. The draw that Miriam needs is less now than before.

It is time to think about marketing. An Advisory Group will help with the revenue enhancement portion of the project. The advisory group doesn't need to be large: Miriam, you, a marketing expert and possibly another small business person who has lived through a business stabilization and growth project.

Because her cash position has improved so much, Miriam may attempt to suspend the turnaround process. This is not the time to abandon the project! Much more needs to be accomplished in order to achieve optimal profitability.

Here is Miriam's Score Card for the week:

MIRIAM'S ART AND FRAME
TURNAROUND SCORE CARD

Description	Week 1 Assessment	Week 2 Planning	Week 3 Cash	Week 4 Expenses	Week 5 Revenue	Week 6 Reassess	Target
Cash in the bank	2,250	3,972	8,707	13,982			$25,000
Accounts Receivable over 90 days old	9,250	9,250	8,100	6,125			1,000
Inventory	12,050	11,130	9,030	8,080			8,000
Sales	4,980	2,320	5,625	6,650			8,000
Total Expenses	3,225	1,640	1,890	1,640			1,800*
Current Ratio	1.0	1.0	1.0	1.1			1.6

*Excludes Rent

OBSERVATIONS ON RESULTS AFTER WEEK 4

- Changes made so far are working.
- You notice great improvements in cash and Accounts Receivable.
- Improvements are made in a short time as indicated in the comparison between week one and week four.
- The one employee termination won't impact expenses until the following pay period.
- There is a temptation to relax because of the improvements made. It is important to stick with the turnaround plan.

CASE II

Knecht Roofing and Construction

You recently spoke to Kevin about his expenses and this is what he shared: He had no idea why he had no cash in the bank when he was always busy. He didn't know the difference between fixed vs. variable expenses.

It's costly to provide lunch for the crew. But the advantage is that the crew stays close to the worksite when lunch is supplied, and Kevin gets more work out of them. He will encourage the crew to bring lunches themselves. Maybe he can take them out for lunch once or twice a month. He should keep experimenting to see what works in expense reduction.

Entertainment expenses are high—especially when so much of it is for his crew. He doesn't know if that brings in more business. The fact that he feels justified paying for lunches and entertainment through the company illustrates his lack of understanding regarding legitimate business expenses. Education is necessary.

Advertising is essential but you don't know if it brings in any business. A weekly ad runs in the weekend sports section of the daily paper. No one mentions the ad when they call requesting information or a bid. But, then again, he doesn't ask them where they got his name. All jobs come through a few general contractors with the exception of an occasional referral.

This expense reduction job is yours as Kevin doesn't know that much about the expense reduction process. You need to keep Kevin focused on what is important this month in getting his business stabilized.

Here is Knecht's Score Card after Week 4:

KNECHT ROOFING AND CONSTRUCTION TURNAROUND SCORE CARD

Description	Week 1 Assessment	Week 2 Planning	Week 3 Cash	Week 4 Expenses	Week 5 Revenue	Week 6 Reassess	Target
Cash in the bank	1,250	2,200	2,950	7,200			$10,000
Accounts Receivable	15,120	16,120	19,620	18,120			7,500
Revenue per job	3,495	3,400	3,550	3,600			4,000
Costs and Expenses per job	3,589	4,050	2,925	2,850			3,000
Jobs Completed	1	1	2	1			3
Net Income	(940)	(650)	1,250	750			3,000
Current Ratio	.3	.3	.3	.4			.5

OBSERVATIONS ON RESULTS AFTER WEEK 4

• Great work was done collecting receivables. The net improvement is over $5,000.

• Expenses in actual dollars per job, has decreased, settling more in line with where it should be.

• The cash position looks better because of improved collection of Accounts Receivable. Also, this week's job was paid with cash.

• Kevin is hurting personally because he hasn't taken a draw for four weeks.

CASE III
Sherwood's SureSave Market and Auto Repair

Expenses were in line with industry averages until the supermarket opened across the street. Now, Sherwood's is cautious because of decreased customer traffic. Adjustments were made and expenses are falling in line.

However, it is still good to track them. Expenses cannot get out of line, until revenue picks up again. They might want to reduce convenience store hours even more in the future although that part of the business will only last a couple more weeks.

If they get out of the gas business, then associated expenses drop and that will improve the income position. They can sell their pumps and tanks to gain cash necessary in the near future to finance remodeling of the convenience store into a showroom for new complementary products.

The Advisory Group met again and confirmed the initial thinking about audio electronics as a great addition to the auto repair shop. The new audio shop will specialize in audio systems for any type of road vehicle—cars, campers, motor homes, etc. Boat owners might be targeted.

During the week you met with some suppliers eager to help you promote their audio products. Some start up and testing expenses are reasonable

The name of the new business will be *Audio Alternatives*. Two people were hired to sell and install the systems. They both have solid experience in the industry and have been great advisors on the best brands to sell.

Signs were placed on the street and on the marquee to advertise *Audio Alternatives*. Initial jobs will begin next week. Special discounts will be offered to loyal customers.

Here is Sherwood's Score Card for the week:

SHERWOOD'S SURESAVE
TURNAROUND SCORE CARD

Description	Week 1 Assessment	Week 2 Planning	Week 3 Cash	Week 4 Expenses	Week 5 Revenue	Week 6 Reassess	Target
Cash	40,602	38,996	47,073	44,186			**$50,000**
Sales – Auto Shop and New	7,750	8,100	7,900	8,137			**35,000**
Sales Gas and Convenience Store	10,285	9,125	7,937	5,902			**0**
Total Costs and Expenses	18,200	23,073	16,733	19,892			**10,000**
Current Ratio	1.3	1.3	1.3	1.2			**1.5**

OBSERVATIONS ON RESULTS AFTER WEEK 4

- Cash has remained pretty constant despite the decrease in sales.

- Total expenses are up because this week was payroll. However, expenses appear to be under control.

- The Advisory Group feels good about audio electronics. The feasibility has been studied and a small electronics inventory has been delivered.

SEVEN

STEP 5
Increasing Revenue

Cash management has improved; expenses are going down big time. Now, the hardest part: getting more sales and revenue through the door. The long-range goal in sales generation is to persuade more customers to spend more money more frequently. The short-term goal is to increase sales any way you can and as quickly as you can.

You have worked through four steps into the turnaround process, which equals four weeks; two weeks remain in the 30-day turnaround timeframe. As a reminder, the model (right) illustrates the sequential steps followed. Now is the time to focus on the revenue-generating portion of the business, taking action immediately to increase revenue this week.

UNIVERSAL TURNAROUND MODEL

MONITORING AND REASSESSING

ASSESSING THE SITUATION

ACCOUNTING INFORMATION
—
ADVISORY GROUP
—
INDUSTRY DATA

INCREASING REVENUE

PLANNING THE TURNAROUND

REDUCING EXPENSES

IMPROVING CASH MANAGEMENT

Of the three major areas of improvement, increasing revenue is the one area where you have the least control. It is much easier to improve cash management and control expenses than to increase sales. Major improvements in revenue cannot be made overnight, but a change in direction can be. Results are hard to see in a week; in fact, changes might not even be seen in a month. But you want sales to improve as quickly as possible.

Revenue must exceed all expenses, including overhead. To know if this is occurring, your accounting system must be accurate and current. In the assessment chapter, the breakeven analysis was completed in order to inform you how much revenue was necessary to cover all expenses. In the last chapter, expenses were discussed and the focus was to breakeven by reducing expenses with no change in revenue.

There are approaches that can be taken that will lead to quick changes in revenue. The breakeven analysis helps bring hard numbers into focus, and those numbers will help you turn the business around.

There are three ways to increase revenue:

1. Secure more sales

2. Secure more customers

3. Increase prices (as most small businesses undervalue their services)

Critical aspects of the sales cycle must be evaluated. Perhaps these aspects were examined during the assessment phase. Evaluations should include examining the number of people walking through the front door, the number of purchases, the percentage of purchasers of those who walk through the door, and possibly the amount of revenue per purchase. Accounting, if done correctly, will reveal this critical information to you.

The available resources are very important in this stage. The accounting information should track critical data from the sales cycle. Industry data allow us to benchmark this business against the best in the industry. The Advisory Group can provide helpful feedback on marketing changes you want to try.

Each of these resources will be used in the building-revenue process. The most important is accounting information. That resource provides information about existing sales, the cost of those sales and important trends regarding the market place.

Another great tool that will help you build revenue is the Geometric Marketing Grid (another use of the four-quadrant grid) shown below. All products and customers are grouped into one of the four quadrants.

GEOMETRIC MARKETING GRID

	Existing Customers	New Customers
Existing Products	I	II
New Products	III	IV

If a business is not growing, it's dying! It is difficult, if not impossible, to remain the same year after year. Things change. The economy improves then worsens. Competitors come and go within the market. New technology and better products are developed. All of a sudden your products might become obsolete or unnecessary.

The business must grow to remain viable. And grow it will with the guidelines in this phase. Certainly, selling more of your existing products to existing customers makes sense, and plans need to be developed to do that. But, linear growth is tedious and slows down over time.

All aspects of your marketing can be categorized into one of the four quadrants. This concept of *geometric growth* is critical to the stabilization and revenue growth of the business. Geometric growth comes from many different angles: existing customers, new customers, existing products, new products.

Keeping current customers satisfied and loyal is important. But you must also acquire new customers. An additional dimension is to persuade both current and future customers to spend more money with you, and more often. Another angle is to develop new products that will appeal to those current and future customers.

Here are some examples:

- **Quadrant I. Sell existing products to existing customers.** This is the base business. Let's imagine you own a cherry orchard. In this business you sell as many cherries as possible to current customers. Hopefully, this means that they will buy more than they are buying now.

- **Quadrant II. Sell existing products to new customers.** Following the cherry orchard example, the goal is to find new customers for the cherries you grow and sell. This may be accomplished by using different marketing strategies, different distribution channels, possibly even finding completely new markets, perhaps overseas. The aim is to sell your cherries to new customers.

- **Quadrant III. Sell new products to existing customers.** Your cherry customers could have need for peaches, pears, apples and possibly many other complementary products to the ones you already sell—maybe canned cherries, cherry juice, or pie tins. Ideally, these new products can also be produced by your orchard. This provides additional sales through new angles.

More revenue is generated with less cost and more speed when new products are sold to existing customers than when existing products are sold to new customers. That is true most of the time. It depends, however, on product development and distribution costs. I assume that distribution costs, in most cases, are more expensive than product-development costs. That makes growth in Quadrant III less expensive than growth in Quadrant II. There is no question that the most expensive growth occurs in Quadrant IV.

- **Quadrant IV. Sell new products to new customers.** This means that you could sell peaches, pears and apples to new customers, and then add cherries to the order as well.

UNDERSTANDING CURRENT PRODUCTS AND CUSTOMERS IN QUADRANT I

I discussed how important marketing is in my first book: *In the BLACK—Nine Principles to Make Your Business Profitable.* Some of those concepts are reviewed here but in a different context. The purpose now is to turn the business around quickly, not just examine effective business principles.

Marketing is the business function that brings customers to your door and culminates in some sort of sale. Great customers do not just appear; they are made.

Look at it this way: You have an amazing product with a great profit margin that people are willing to pay for. Would you stop telling people about it? Marketing informs customers about your products and brings them through the door.

EVERYTHING YOU DO IN BUSINESS IS RELATED TO MARKETING.

Accounting should play an integral part of the marketing effort. How can an accounting system help in marketing? Your accounting system should collect critical information that is evaluated by the business operator. Your accounting system should provide answers to the following questions which will promote sales growth:

What products and services are selling right now? Are they profitable?

What products are returned, and why?

Are there some products that you should not sell because they are outdated or no longer meet customer needs, or perhaps they are no longer profitable?

What are customers buying? Where are they coming from? How much did each customer pay for the products and services you provide? How did they pay—cash or credit?

What product lines are selling the most? What products have the greatest gross profit margin? How are these products selling compared to other products? If financed, is there a correlation between the products sold on credit and bad debts?

What information from each sale needs to be collected to help in making future sales and in responding to customers' specific needs?

CUSTOMER SERVICE ANALYSIS (QUADRANTS I AND III)

Some sales may be good for the business but not for the customer. You might benefit from short-term profits, but long-term customer relationships could be damaged. This can be true when you reduce quality without lowering prices or when you knowingly take advantage of customers.

- Every customer has different needs. Ask for the customer's point of view. What pain does your product or service relieve? What need does it fulfill? Then, express your point of view and decide how the sale will meet and exceed both parties' needs.

- Major customer motivators are health, wealth, and happiness. I have heard this expressed also as time, money and peace of mind. Whatever their motivation, demonstrate to customers how your products provide benefits for which they are searching.

Yes, sales must be profitable. Customer needs must also be met. And there must be a balance between the two. Don't ruin your most effective and least expensive marketing tool: word-of-mouth advertising. It can lead to your success or demise overnight.

Here are some questions that can help in your customer analysis:

Who are the major customers and what do they want from you?

What do you sell? How does that product or service meet your customers' needs? How do you get customers to your door so you can show them your product or service?

What can be learned from your customers about how to better meet their needs? What other products and services do they need that is provided right now with minimum effort?

What would customers change about your product or service?

How are you seen compared to your competition?

What about customer service?

If it is a commodity you sell, how can you add value or differentiate it from the competition?

What does the business look like when a customer approaches?

How is the customer approached when he or she enters/calls the business?

Should a customer be a member of your Advisory Group? (Sure!)

The answers to these questions add to your data bank of what you know about Quadrant I customers.

KEEP YOUR CURRENT CUSTOMERS—THEY COMPRISE YOUR BASE BUSINESS.

Your base business comes from Quadrant I. It is important to understand what is happening with products and services in that quadrant.

Statistics show that it is much less costly to keep customers you already have than it is to find new ones. Once you have customers, you want to develop their loyalty so they will never want to go elsewhere for the products and services they currently buy from you.

A two-pronged attack is essential for dealing with existing customers. You must keep them happy with what they are buying from you already. Also, you want them to spend more money with you, more often. These are the two critical objectives of a successful marketing plan for your business.

Customer service is imperative in keeping customers satisfied and loyal. It is a true differentiator in the market place.

Develop plans to have existing customers spend more money with your business. These questions will help you:

What else do customers need that you can provide?

Is there any way that you can alter the arrangement to include a regular monthly payment?

How can you increase residual sales or repeat sales?

Will they buy more of your existing products and services?

How can you motivate them to spend more money, more often?

What types of complementary products and services could you offer existing customers that would help them more effectively meet their needs?

Here are guidelines for improving customer relations with your Quadrant I customers:

- Meet or exceed agreed-upon customer expectations 100% of the time. The key words are agreed upon. Customer expectations continually change so expectations must be set early in the relationship so that, as a business, you can exceed them.

- Develop the concept of *customer loyalty* in all of your customers. This is done through constant communication with them about their needs, and how your products and services are meeting those needs. Customer loyalty is a customer who continues to buy from you, no matter what outside forces may try to capture this business.

- Develop processes for dealing with customers consistently and promptly. Customers are fickle; one bad experience can erase a lot of good ones. Each transaction must be handled as if it were the very first transaction with that particular customer.

Now you must consider what you can do right now—today, this week, or this month in order to get your customer base to spend more money with our business?

Every customer is a new customer. What works with one customer may not work with the next. Great sales people identify the needs and points of view of each new customer before they give the customers their personal point of view. Then they meet the customers' needs with the products and services they are selling. These skills can be learned and transferred to others during sales meetings and training.

DEVELOP NEW CUSTOMERS IN QUADRANTS II AND IV

Let's discuss getting new customers next. Development in both Quadrants II and IV is expensive—more expensive than developing more sales in Quadrant I. However, sometimes Quadrant I customers are just tapped out. They have purchased everything that they possibly can from you. You must move to new quadrants for growth.

As I stated, I am never happy with my business unless it is growing. It is an imperative goal to grow and continually increase your customer base. Here are some questions that I have found helpful in analyzing how to attract more customers:

What new products and services do you need to develop to attract new customers?

What kind of marketing research data do you have on which to make your marketing and product development decisions?

How can you customize your products and services for each new customer as they want?

How can you improve a prospective customer's awareness of your products and services without spending much time educating them? Education is much more time-consuming than marketing; you want to stick with marketing as much as possible.

DEVELOP NEW PRODUCTS IN QUADRANTS III AND IV

The concept here is to develop new products that your existing customers and new customers can use. Developing new products can take a long time—too long to help in this critical turnaround project.

But, you could offer complementary products from other vendors. For instance, before convenience stores were on every corner, a gas station client of mine placed a used cooler in his front showroom and started selling soda. Within a week, he covered the cost of the cooler and was selling more gas to boot.

New product development is critical in the growth strategies of your business. Here are questions that help with that analysis:

What products are customers asking your sales people for that you do not currently provide?

Is it practical to develop these as new products?

Does new technology exist that could change the marketplace significantly, in the near future, and can you adopt these into your own product lines?

What trends do you notice in the marketplace that might affect what you will do or not do in the near future?

EVERY BUSINESS ASSET AND EMPLOYEE SHOULD RELATE TO REVENUE GENERATION

Every asset should be engaged in making sales. Everyone in the company must have a marketing mindset! Every employee must be involved in the sales process in some way. If he is not involved on the front line with customers, then he should be supporting someone who is.

Sales training is essential! Call a sales meeting often to determine what is working and what is not. Discuss changes in sales techniques to enhance everyone's skills. Include the office and production staff in sales meetings, listen to their input, and remind them that sales make the business flourish. Sales meetings should address improving the sales skills of all employees dealing with outside customers.

QUICK STEPS TO MORE REVENUE

How can you increase revenue immediately, this week, next week, etc?

• Conduct an inventory clearance sale

• Print and distribute flyers advertising a great one-time sale.

- Cross-promote your products and services with other businesses in the area.

- Give your coupons to the other stores if you are in a retail shopping mall.

- Consider lowering credit requirements.

- Try trade shows and flea markets.

- Raise prices and hope for an increase in dollar volume. Usually, a 5% increase in price will go unnoticed.

- Lower your prices and hope for more volume which will offset lower prices.

- Keep prices the same and increase the use of promotions, advertising, and rebates.

- Secret shop your competition to see what they are doing. Then offer more value than your competition.

- Make special one-time offers with great incentives.

- Change the appearance of the business. Sometimes this will cause more and curious new customers to check you out. This can work rapidly, particularly in retail.

- Offer promotions with neighboring businesses or associates.

- Change advertising promotions. Promotions don't work forever; they need to change often.

- Some products cost a lot to produce and sell. Drop them from your product line and focus on products with the highest margins.

When you try anything new or different, be sure to document your results.

Frequently Asked Questions

Is growth essential to business health?

Yes! And with worldwide competition, perhaps diversity in products and services is essential as well.

Why isn't marketing the first step in the turnaround process?

Marketing is the hardest area of the business to control. Controlling cash and reducing expenses are both hard, but they are internally controlled. You can impact those areas today while increasing sales could take longer.

SUMMARY – WHERE YOU SHOULD BE AT THIS POINT

You completed an evaluation of all products and services offered by the business to ensure that each is profitable by itself and that the margins for each product meet certain criteria. This may have been done or partially done during the assessment phase, but it is complete now. You feel that all your products are currently viable in the marketplace.

You completed an evaluation of customer service within the company, getting ideas from several customers implementing the ideas that made sense. You will be implementing new products and services that will meet their continually growing needs.

You know what your base business is and what it will look like over the next year. You have a better feeling for your products, customers, and employees.

You completed an evaluation of the Geometric Marketing Model and implemented strategies from that analysis to increase sales and revenue.

Be sure to document your test results. This will ensure that you learn marketing lessons the first time so you can apply them in the future.

CHAPTER SEVEN
INCREASING REVENUE
Key Learning Points

- The goal in sales generation is to attract more customers to spend more money, more frequently in your business. The short-term goal is to increase sales any way you can as quickly as you can.

- This step is the most difficult of the three execution steps because you have the least control. Generally cash and expenses are controllable internally. But sales are not. That is why this is the last step.

- Usually Profit Experts are the least experienced in this step: increasing revenue. Thus, the primer in this book is very helpful in advancing up the marketing learning curve quickly.

- An understanding of the Geometric Marketing Model is essential in understanding the business. The base business is in Quadrant I. Stabilization work is mostly done in this quadrant. However, future growth will occur in the other three quadrants.

- An understanding of products and services is also important. The purpose of each product and service is examined from the customer's point of view. It is also critical to know the demand for each product and service and the margin or contribution the sale of each product and service gives the company.

- Customers are a great source of information. Consider ways to acquire feedback about products and services that could be made into quick sales improvements.

CASE I
Miriam's Art and Frame Shop

You have worked on cash management and expense control. Now it is time to increase revenue. Fluctuation does occur in this business, and it's a trait to which you will need to adjust. Overall sales have been constant but well below your target of $8,000 a week.

You have always depended on customers coming into the shop. That still works. In fact, a builder came in this week looking for artwork for new construction. You will be working on a proposal for him.

Other ideas for increasing revenue are being considered. The Advisory Group discussed these ideas:

- Analyze the product mix and push for more profitable products. Ensure that each product's margins are adequate. That may have been handled in the expense section but seems appropriate here as well.

- Develop a new line of products that can be sold on the internet and in retail (Quadrants III and IV).

- Send flyers each month to customers (special sales) promoting discount pricing for the month (Quadrant I).

- Raise prices by 10%. Miriam hasn't had a price increase in three years. If you are not losing business due to pricing, you are priced too low.

- Demonstrate new projects on the website suggesting decorating ideas.

All ideas will be tested this week to see what works and what doesn't. Those that work will become standard products and services in the store.

This is Miriam's Score Card for the week:

MIRIAM'S ART AND FRAME TURNAROUND SCORE CARD

Description	Week 1 Assessment	Week 2 Planning	Week 3 Cash	Week 4 Expenses	Week 5 Revenue	Week 6 Reassess	Target
Cash in the bank	2,250	3,972	8,707	13,982	16,672		**$25,000**
Accounts Receivable over 90 days old	9,250	9,250	8,100	6,125	3,925		**1,000**
Inventory	12,050	11,130	9,030	8,080	8,005		**8,000**
Sales	4,980	2,320	5,625	6,650	5,925		**8,000**
Total Expenses	3,225	1,640	1,890	1,640	3,640		**1,800***
Current Ratio	1.0	1.0	1.0	1.1	1.1		**1.6**

*Excludes Rent

OBSERVATIONS ON RESULTS AFTER WEEK 5

- Cash continues to improve. This is because of collections on Accounts receivable accounts and more cash sales.
- More regular payments being made by active clients.
- Inventory has stabilized near the target. That is a big success in the turnaround project.
- Expenses continue to rise higher than forecast. This might be because of an inaccurate forecast or because production expense continues to be high. Piece-meal costing was forecast but has not yet been implemented.
- Sales will continue to improve with implementation of recommendations from this step.
- Again, the huge improvement in cash may tempt Miriam to discontinue the implementation of the Turnaround Business Plan. Vigilance is key to success.

CASE II

Knecht's Roofing and Construction

Your primary recommendation is that Kevin increase profit margins by raising all bids by 15%. Margins are up on the jobs Kevin has accepted. The number of bids going out is the same but the number of accepted bids has dropped somewhat.

Where he was getting 95% of his bids accepted, now about 40% of his bids are accepted—but they are all profitable. This was predicted when prices were raised. Kevin is making a concerted effort to make more bids.

No wonder he had so much work before: he was always the low bidder; buyers were satisfied with his work and delighted with his prices. There was good reason to be delighted with his prices given he wasn't making any money.

Still two jobs a week are completed. The goal is three jobs a week so that Kevin can take his draw and the business remain profitable.

If it appears that 40% of all bids are accepted, then one way to raise revenue is to increase the number of bids presented. That would lead to more jobs accepted at satisfactory margin rates. Perhaps there might be some margin slippage in slow business periods such as winter. The purpose of that strategy is to keep everyone employed so that crews are intact when business picks up. It is not a permanent strategy.

For the longer-term, Kevin is preparing to join the local Home Builders Association, meet with five new building contractors, and look for referrals from recent customers. He hired someone to hand out flyers door-to-door in a fifteen year-old neighborhood, one that is prime for new roofs.

In reality, at this stage of the turnaround process Kevin is doing fairly well as far as revenue generation is concerned.

This is Kevin's Score Card at the end of Week 5:

KNECHT ROOFING AND CONSTRUCTION
TURNAROUND SCORE CARD

Description	Week 1 Assessment	Week 2 Planning	Week 3 Cash	Week 4 Expenses	Week 5 Revenue	Week 6 Reassess	Target
Cash in the bank	1,250	2,200	2,950	7,200	8,850		$10,000
Accounts Receivable	15,120	16,120	19,620	18,120	15,120		7,500
Revenue per job	3,495	3,400	3,550	3,600	3,850		4,000
Costs and Expenses per job	3,589	4,050	2,925	2,850	3,025		3,000
Jobs Completed	1	1	2	1	2		3
Net Income	(940)	(650)	1,250	750	1,650		3,000
Current Ratio	.3	.3	.3	.4	.4		.5

OBSERVATIONS ON RESULTS AFTER WEEK 5

- Net income has improved. That is because Kevin only accepts jobs that are profitable.

- Revenue per job is improving because of increased prices and better bidding.

- Costs are nearing the target. In fact, if they stayed where they are right now, everyone would be happy.

- Kevin still needs to average one more job per week.

- Kevin is taking no draw as yet. That will occur next week for the first time. He can support himself and possibly catch up on payments for his four-wheelers and other toys.

CASE III

Sherwood's SureSave and Auto Repair

Cash has improved. This is because sales in the auto repair side of the business increased even as convenience store sales dropped to zero. The convenience store actually closed this week while the display room was constructed for Audio Alternatives. Advertising *Audio Alternatives* attracted more customers to the auto repair side of the business.

Flyers offering *Audio Alternatives* incentives were sent to existing customers; many also came in for auto repairs. This made you aware that there was room for revenue expansion in the auto repair side of the business even though you were expecting most of the business growth on the electronics side.

Convenience store employees are leaving since they are not trained in vehicle audio systems. They like to listen but can't sell electronics effectively. And it takes some special training to sell audio systems.

The initial sales testing of the audio systems went remarkably well thanks to training by the system supplier. The new employees proved themselves adept at selling and installing the systems. The system supplier is surprised and pleased with the initial success of the new venture.

It appears that this venture will eventually replace and outgrow the net income lost from the convenience store and gasoline sales, which had lower margins than the new digital audio products.

A big thank you to the Advisory Group for brainstorming ideas leading to the property's audio store addition!

This is Sherwood's Score Card for the week:

SHERWOOD'S SURESAVE
TURNAROUND SCORE CARD

Description	Week 1 Assessment	Week 2 Planning	Week 3 Cash	Week 4 Expenses	Week 5 Revenue	Week 6 Reassess	Target
Cash	40,602	38,996	47,073	44,186	56,456		**$50,000**
Sales – Auto Shop and New Audio	7,750	8,100	7,900	8,137	12,123		**35,000**
Sales Gas and Convenience Store	10,285	9,125	7,937	5,902	1,988		**0**
Total Costs and Expenses	18,200	23,073	16,733	19,892	8,788		**10,000**
Current Ratio	1.3	1.3	1.3	1.2	1.2		**1.5**

OBSERVATIONS ON RESULTS AFTER WEEK 5

- Cash has improved. There was no payroll this week and no depreciation.

- Total revenue is up because of a special sale to existing customers of entertainment systems for automobiles and other vehicles.

- Expenses are under control. The expense line will increase as the electronics part of the business gets going. Inventory will also expand.

- Gasoline sales are dead. The convenience store is closed.

- The early *Audio Alternatives* test appears to be successful.

EIGHT

STEP 6
Monitoring and Reassessing

Five steps in the six-step turnaround model have been addressed. Not everything has gone perfectly, but enough progress has been made to keep the business moving forward.

Cash management has improved, expenses reduced and revenue increased—at least all areas are improving. The business is not out of the woods yet, by any means, but it is advancing.

In Step 1 you performed the original assessment and decided that with some changes the business could achieve stabilization and, with the help of the turnaround project, become viable and profitable.

A solid turnaround plan was developed with the help of key people including employees and an Advisory Group. Action steps were taken in three major areas:

- Cash management. All cash outlays, in particular, were approved by the business owner or you in your role as accountant and controller. You also stepped up the Account Receivable collection efforts.

- Expense reduction. All expenses were thoroughly examined to determine the necessity and the timing of each. Not all expense reduction ideas can be implemented in 30 days so some are still in the process of being implemented.

- Revenue generation. Geometric marketing was the focus here. An analysis was made of all products and services to see where the profits were coming from and what other programs might be implemented quickly to generate revenue. Sales benchmarks were set.

The twenty-five days have been exciting and challenging. Maybe you have fewer people. Maybe you have fewer products. Maybe you have new and different relationships with suppliers and customers. And the business is more profitable.

The Universal Score Card looks better. The business has stabilized and things are more under control. It is once again time for you to use your Profit Expert skills to monitor and reassess the situation—the sixth step in the Universal Turnaround Model as illustrated below:

UNIVERSAL TURNAROUND MODEL

MONITORING AND REASSESSING

ASSESSING THE SITUATION

ACCOUNTING INFORMATION
—
ADVISORY GROUP
—
INDUSTRY DATA

INCREASING REVENUE

PLANNING THE TURNAROUND

REDUCING EXPENSES

IMPROVING CASH MANAGEMENT

In Step 6—Monitoring and Reassessing is time to ensure that new or enhanced systems are working and that they are accurately monitored. This is not a relaxing week by any means. It is time to review the five weeks of project implementation to evaluate that initial assessment and compare it with the business's current position.

The **Universal Score Card** created during the assessment and business planning phases has provided a great way to monitor progress. As you can see from the generic Score Card below, key indicators are monitored within each of the three major elements—cash management, expense reduction, revenue enhancement— during the turnaround process.

The reassessment phase focuses on evaluating where the business is right now compared to where it was five weeks ago. What has been accomplished? How close are you to the target score card targets after six weeks?

UNIVERSAL SCORE CARD MODEL (EXAMPLE)

Description	Week 1 Assessment	Week 2 Planning	Week 3 Cash	Week 4 Expenses	Week 5 Revenue	Week 6 Reassess	Target
Cash in the bank							
Accounts Receivable over 30/90 days old							
Bills (cash) owed in the next week							
End of Month Accounting ratios							
Weekly Sales							
Monthly Sales							
Cash Sales vs. Credit							
Number of jobs							
Revenue per job							

Cash, expenses, and revenue (the three major elements emphasized in the turnaround process) are all monitored from a glance at the Score Card. Remember, that what gets monitored and measured usually improves. The important columns for analysis this week are the Week 6 Reassessment against the target column on the far right. How close are the actual results to the target?

You can see that positive changes have occurred. Improvements have been made and now the business is running better. It is time to evaluate what happened during the first five steps of the **Universal Turnaround Model.**

Now it is time to check the validity of your initial assumptions and recommendations. There is still time to pull out of the business entirely and do something else. So, let's re-examine the situation. Keep in mind that your focus was on a quick turnaround—things that could be accomplished in 30 days or less with a small businesses having less than 20 employees.

It's probably time for celebration. The business has survived the 30 days and is doing better. That celebration can happen in many ways: dinner with the business owners and their spouses at a nice restaurant, a weekend getaway at a nice resort or maybe a cost-effective work party.

MONITORING

The Score Card, which you have used throughout all the phases, is the most important tool for monitoring the business to make sure it is progressing toward the turnaround goals.

Monitoring requires both the Profit Expert and business owner to scrutinize, at least weekly, business progress. The Score Card was designed for your particular business monitors key measures of success. Monitoring also requires that you determine if your initial assessment was accurate, the Turnaround Business Plan working and recommendations implemented.

Monitoring also includes a quick look at cash, expenses, and revenue for the week. The Score Card has allowed you to monitor key information ensuring the business is moving in the right direction. It illustrates the importance of maintaining critical, up-to-date accounting information as most of the Score Card indicators come directly from the accounting system.

The Score Card and other tools have enabled you to adequately monitor the business's progress. Perhaps the most important of those tools is the business owner's heightened awareness what is truly important.

The Score Card also allows you to quickly recognize trends and potential problems, making quick adjustments where possible to keep the business moving forward. Trends are spotted in each of the three cases at the end of this chapter. Some are more evident than others but improvement has been made in all cases.

This is also a good time, because of turnaround success, to remind the owner that you are committed to the business for a year. Stabilization is not enough; long-term growth is the goal, and you can assist in that regard.

The Score Card will be used in the future but will change according to the client's needs. It is not just a turnaround tool but a good management tool as well and will be used regularly.

REASSESSING

It is also time to reflect and assess the business's current status. This isn't much different from the first assessment outlined in Chapter Three. The process is essentially the same although the starting point is different. Ultimately the snapshot of the business will be different as well.

The critical aspect of this step is to reassess where the business currently is and make plans for the next 30 days and beyond. This 30-

day intensive process has not solved all the business's problems but progress has definitely been made. There are many more problems to solve and some of the same ones will probably return later.

Some of the changes may not have worked as well as expected, and perhaps the business is in worse shape than you originally thought. But, some minor improvements have been made. Receiving feedback that a sick child is improving is better than no feedback at all. Small improvements can lead to big successes.

A great Advisory Group was established and will continue to meet. The group includes experts with valuable information including a customer who has provided a unique perspective. The Advisory Group gave first-rate counsel in making the business better in just 30 days.

Below are more critical questions that need to be answered now:

Do you move on or withdraw from the business?

You can still tell the business owner it's not working. If you can't see the light, back out now. You know a lot more about the business than you did just a few weeks ago. If this is the case, you might want to skip the celebration mentioned above.

What is working well in the business?

What is the new business model? How is it working? How has the model changed since the turnaround process began?

What is not working well in the business?

The answers might not be as severe as they were during the first assessment but there are always processes and products that can be improved. The answers to these questions are critical to the success of the reassessing phases.

The first month the Score Card focused on survival indicators, and you monitored that Score Card almost daily. Now things have changed. While there are still many recommendations that need to be implemented, the business is moving from stabilization to growth mode, even if only slightly. So, the Score Card will change somewhat. You will monitor different indicators in the future.

Here are some possible changes:

UNIVERSAL SCORE CARD EXAMPLE
(As the business goes beyond the reassessing step)

Description	Week 1 Assessment	Week 2 Planning	Week 3 Cash	Week 4 Expenses	Week 5 Revenue	Week 6 Reassess	Target
CASH							
Cash in bank							
Accounts Rec over 30 days							
Bills owed in next month							
EXPENSES							
Payroll as % of Sales							
Production Standards							
Number of hours worked							
Accounting Ratios							
SALES							
Sales this wk							
Sales this mth							
Sales YTD							

What about the must-have versus the like-to-have indicators? Other possible additions to the Score Card include:

- Sales per day per sales person
- Advertising spent as % of sales
- Gross profit margin
- Production standards
- Average purchase amount
- Billable days
- Billable hours
- Etc.

REMEMBER: WHAT YOU MONITOR AND MEASURE IMPROVES!

The Score Card will change over time as different indicators become important. The Score Card established for the turnaround project was designed for monitoring each week. Now the timing might change. Perhaps certain indicators will be monitored on a monthly basis, perhaps on a quarterly basis. Sales forecasts are the most important indicators and should be monitored frequently. At other times, perhaps the expense category becomes the most critical to monitor.

Everything on the Score Card can be found in the accounting information which is the card's best resource for data during the six-step process.

RESOURCE HELP

As stated before, the Universal Turnaround Model illustrates six important steps in the turnaround process and in general business growth. The center of the model illustrates three great resources that you have used throughout the process in each of the turnaround steps. They are important again in this reassessment phase of the project.

ACCOUNTING INFORMATION

This has been the most important information available on which to make decisions during the turnaround project. All the indicators on the Score Card come from the accounting system. The importance of keeping information up-to-date is paramount, especially when you are making decisions about the next phase of the company's growth.

INDUSTRY DATA

Comparison data always provides information to which you can compare your results and status. It might not be as important as accounting information but it is an invaluable resource to have during any reassessment step.

ADVISORY GROUP

The small group of advisors can continue to offer wisdom beyond the data! They can be very astute when reassessing the business at the end of the six steps. Eventually, you will gain wisdom as well. But the initial purpose of the group continues to be the same: provide expertise that complements your accounting expertise and the expertise provided by the business owner.

Frequently Asked Questions

What if there are no meaningful changes during the 30 day turnaround period?

Then you are probably out of business!

What if you decide it's time to liquidate?

If the business has value or if the assets or inventory have value, sell them. Never liquidate unless the assets are worth more than the business.

How can you tell when you are finished?

You are probably never finished. The business is stabilized but growth brings a new set of problems. Monitoring what is happening and continually assessing the environment are important in dealing with the never-ending supply of problems that arise.

How could you make planning and each of the other turnaround phases more effective next time?

The six-step process works. Experience is what makes them work even better. As you develop as a Profit Expert, you will gain expertise in implementing the six-step turnaround process.

What can you learn from the original assessment completed some weeks ago? This whole thing was a real pain in the butt. Will it be easier next time?

Your experience and expertise will make this reassessment less difficult.

Do you go through the same six steps again the next 30 days?

Probably. The situation might be different but the process is the same. I am sure that not all the problems have been solved just yet. Perhaps you will have action steps in all three improvement areas going on simultaneously.

It seems like you are in survival mode every month in this business? Can you ever get ahead?

If you have survived the first month, then the second month will probably be easier. The turnaround steps demonstrated in *Red to Black in 30 Days* are to be used every month until the business is stabilized and growing steadily. Sleep then comes more easily at night.

SUMMARY—WHERE YOU SHOULD BE AT THIS POINT

This step focuses on monitoring changes made and reassessing the situation. The six turnaround steps should be completed by the end of this 30-day period.

That doesn't mean that everything is wonderful, but at least the business survived and can now work on thriving. Essentially, the six steps are completed and the reassessment will lead into a new iteration of change. The **Universal Turnaround Model** steps can be used again.

An effective monitoring system is in place to track important business indicators. The important indicators are monitored on the Score Card that was specifically designed for this business. This reflects that a good accounting system is in place providing needed information for the Score Card.

An evaluation was completed of the 30-day turnaround project. Certainly this reassessment resembles the first step of our turnaround cycle which is implemented once again, this time with growth rather than survival as the main goal. This leads to new directions for the business.

As the accountant, you and the business owner should take time to reflect on the turnaround process, documenting what went well and what could have been improved. Overall, you should have a much better handle on how the business runs and the viability of the business model as well as the commitment of the people involved.

CHAPTER EIGHT
MONITORING AND REASSESSING
Key Learning Points

- Monitoring is critical for new or revised systems to ensure they are working the way they were intended to work.

- The reassessment should include critical questions much like the initial assessment work. What is working well? What is not working well? How is the business situated compared to where it was five weeks ago?

- Once a reassessment is complete, future business growth needs to be addressed. Where is the business heading? Where are the areas of growth in the near future? You should be moving from stabilization to growth. This reassessment will lead into another iteration of business improvement.

- Overall, you and the business owner have a much better handle on how the business runs, the viability of the business model and the commitment of the people involved.

CASE I
Miriam's Art and Frame Shop

Cash is under control.

The kids are off the credit cards. No cash is used to support other businesses. And, most importantly, the siphoning of cash from the business by the old bookkeeper has stopped; she is gone and cash is no longer disappearing. Some changes were made quite quickly. The criminality of the bookkeeper's actions is under consideration. The critical project is continuing to get the business turned around quickly and on the right track. The business is stabilizing and growth is in the future.

While business may be stable, this is not the time to lay back and rest! Many problems still exist in the business and lack of growth is a big one! Cash is under control but not abundant by any means. Sales and revenue need to increase. Expenses are under control and appear at the minimum level given the amount of sales that are occurring.

Miriam's Score Card is in place and will not change during the next iteration of change. But, in the reassessment, increasing revenue and sales are the areas needing improvement.

The focus of the new business plan is on increasing revenue and on discovering new tactics and strategies that will increase sales while keeping expenses at a minimum.

Miriam had a big celebration at the end of the turnaround process. All five employees, spouses and you went out to celebrate and re-commit to the business's success.

You are getting closer to the Score Card targets than you were 30 days ago. The next iteration of business improvement is more of the same as not all the targets were achieved.

Miriam's Art and Frame has survived the first iteration and is still in business.

It will be around for a long time.

This is Miriam's Score Card for the week:

MIRIAM'S ART AND FRAME TURNAROUND SCORE CARD

Description	Week 1 Assessment	Week 2 Planning	Week 3 Cash	Week 4 Expenses	Week 5 Revenue	Week 6 Reassess	Target
Cash in the bank	2,250	3,972	8,707	13,982	16,672	22,250	**$25,000**
Accounts Receivable over 90 days old	9,250	9,250	8,100	6,125	3,925	1,075	**1,000**
Inventory	12,050	11,130	9,030	8,080	8,005	8,115	**8,000**
Sales	4,980	2,320	5,625	6,650	5,925	7,630	**8,000**
Total Expenses	3,225	1,640	1,890	1,640	3,640	1,740	**1,800***
Current Ratio	1.0	1.0	1.0	1.1	1.1	1.2	**1.6**

*Excludes Rent

OBSERVATIONS ON RESULTS AFTER WEEK 6

- Miriam's Art and Frame Shop survived the six week turnaround process, is more stable and is ready for a growth spurt.

- Not all Score Card targets were reached, but the indicators improved. It is time to get ready for the next iteration of business improvement.

- Continued vigilant work in collecting receivables is necessary.

- Now is the time to determine your percentage of the profits since it will exceed your $1,000 monthly retainer.

- This was truly re-energizing and motivating.

- Miriam's business is viable and profitable and will be even more profitable in the future.
- It is time to create a revised business plan for the next 30 days.

The updated business plan will focus on revenue growth in each of the four geometric marketing quadrants.

The accountant's role is well-defined in the next iteration of business improvement. Your job is to continue the improvement process and document what you have learned and what the business learned during this six-week turnaround process.

This business perfectly fits our criteria of being a small business capable of turning around quickly if the right changes and adjustments are made.

CASE II

Knecht Roofing and Construction

Knecht's Roofing is still in a lot of trouble. The owner, Kevin Knecht learned valuable financial lessons but it will take more time to straighten out this mess. Stabilization is still the major concern—before any profitable growth can occur. It was good that his wife had a job with insurance benefits.

Key issues remain:

- Project margins improved with the higher bids. More work has aided the improvement

- Cash is more in control; there is just not a lot of it to go around.

He certainly has better control of his expenses and a better understanding of what his margins should be in his bids. It is great to have a lot of work, but it is even better to have profitable work. Most of his work, although plentiful, was not profitable.

The reassessment indicated that improvements were made in expense control and margins were increased in the bids that were submitted.

Things look better. Accounts receivable are much lower but collection requires constant attention. Kevin may need a financial planner to work on managing cash but he can take a $1,000 draw every week that he completes three jobs.

As an accountant, you worked 30 hours for a $3,500 roof. That will be coming in the next month.

Here is Kevin's Score Card for this week:

KNECHT ROOFING AND CONSTRUCTION
TURNAROUND SCORE CARD

Description	Week 1 Assessment	Week 2 Planning	Week 3 Cash	Week 4 Expenses	Week 5 Revenue	Week 6 Reassess	Target
Cash in the bank	1,250	2,200	2,950	7,200	8,850	13,100	$10,000
Accounts Receivable	15,120	16,120	19,620	18,120	15,120	11,620	7,500
Revenue per job	3,495	3,400	3,550	3,600	3,850	4,033	4,000
Costs and Expenses per job	3,589	4,050	2,925	2,850	3,025	2,983	3,000
Jobs Completed	1	1	2	1	2	3	3
Net Income	(940)	(650)	1,250	750	1,650	3,150	3,000
Current Ratio	.3	.3	.3	.4	.4	.4	.5*

*Current ratio goal for next iteration is 1.0

OBSERVATIONS ON RESULTS AFTER WEEK 6

- Accounts Receivable continues to improve thus making the cash position better each week.
- Completing three jobs this week made a great difference in net income and cash in the bank.
- He can take a draw this week.

The updated business plan will focus on the following issues:

- Profitable growth—This business is still on shaky ground. It has improved dramatically but still has significant problems. It can and should grow but it can only be profitable growth. Bids and margins need continual scrutinizing.

- Profitable strategies and tactics—These should be on a smaller scale and a more controllable level. Margins must increase. If total revenue goes down, so be it, especially if profit goes up.

This case is a typical case that you will encounter as a small business accountant. Improvements were made in 30 days but this business is nowhere near where it needs to be. It can still go out of business if Kevin returns to his old management tactics.

CASE III

Sherwood's SureSave

Sherwood's is still insulated because of the cash they have in the bank. I wish that everyone could be so lucky.

This cash advantage allows them several months to literally change the business model from one dependent on a convenience store with gasoline sales to one dependent on auto repair and different retail sales. The new business model will focus on the installation of sound systems in all types of vehicles.

The convenience store converts into a showroom for *Audio Alternatives*. The installation work will be done in the bays behind the store where the repair work is done now. The new business plan will focus on the transition time into the new business model. The gasoline tanks, pumps and other equipment have been dismantled.

Initial indications illustrate that the convenience store conversion to electronics will be successful and quickly profitable. You will concede the grocery and gas business to the supermarket across the street but will take advantage of the increased traffic building your own complementary auto repair business at the same intersection.

Because of necessary construction on the property to change the convenience store to an audio and electronics store, no noticeable improvements in cash and business performance are expected as they attempt to finance most of the construction from internal cash flow. The new store will not be complete for another couple of months.

Although decisions are made about the long-term business model for their property, more analysis needs to be done concerning specific marketing plans. All four quadrants are still being analyzed within the framework of the new business model regarding opportunities for expansion. What other new products should be included in the store? How will new customers be attracted to the store? What other services can be offered that will bring customers to the business?

The Sherwoods realize that these business changes are necessary. Business had been stagnant for years; the supermarket across the street caught them by surprise and they were slow to respond. It's hard to see old ways end but these changes guarantee the business will survive into the next generation of Sherwoods.

The Score Card looks like this:

SHERWOOD'S SURESAVE TURNAROUND SCORE CARD

Description	Week 1 Assessment	Week 2 Planning	Week 3 Cash	Week 4 Expenses	Week 5 Revenue	Week 6 Reassess	Target
Cash	40,602	38,996	47,073	44,186	56,456	65,417	**$50,000**
Sales – Auto Shop and New Audio	7,750	8,100	7,900	8,137	12,123	19,997	**35,000**
Sales Gas and Convenience Store	10,285	9,125	7,937	5,902	1,988	0	**0**
Total Costs and Expenses	18,200	23,073	16,733	19,892	8,788	11,036	**10,000**
Current Ratio	1.3	1.3	1.3	1.2	1.2	1.4	**1.5**

OBSERVATIONS ON RESULTS AFTER WEEK 6

- Sales are up $6,000 because of the new audio products and more interest in the auto repair business in the back. A $4,000 audio system installation in a motor home was the primary cause of the increase.

- Expenses are up because of new inventory and the beginning of construction. Expenses will continue to rise because of remodeling.

- Cash is strong as it always has been.

The new business plan will focus on continued growth in both the auto repair business and the audio electronics business. The business has weathered the storm and is poised for growth into the next generation of Sherwoods.

NINE

It's Working!
Now You Are an Expert

Congratulations on the completed turnaround project! You are not quite done, but close.

This chapter focuses on the **DOCUMENT** phase of the **Universal Project Management Model.** With continual improvement as an overarching framework, documentation now becomes the primary objective. You must somehow capture, in writing or with software, the major learning points from the project you experienced during the last several weeks.

Red to Black in 30 Days is based on the continual improvement model first presented in the Introduction and then fully explained in subsequent chapters. You gained business wisdom along the way to become a better accountant and Profit Expert. Now, with your expertise in turnaround projects, you can manage larger and tougher projects, and you can make more money.

Why documentation is important

The continual improvement process provides you a moment to reflect on what you have learned as a Profit Expert during the turnaround project. The turnaround allows you to document the business expertise and wisdom you learned so you can apply it to future turnaround projects.

Document major learning points in two areas:

The specific business turnaround situation.

This will allow you, in the future, to better advise other businesses in similar turnaround circumstances.

And *your unique accounting practice.*

This will allow you to expand and grow your own accounting practice.

The continual improvement concept is illustrated in the **Universal Project Management** model you have seen before:

UNIVERSAL PROJECT MANAGEMENT MODEL

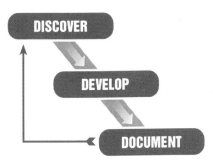

As mentioned before, *Red to Black in 30 Days* closely follows the model. The Table of Contents illustrates that this book is divided into these same three sections. A quick review is in order.

DISCOVER

As a review, the DISCOVER step is the time in which you assess and brainstorm the situation. Here, you determine just what is happening in the business, identifying problems that need to be solved and urgent situations that need to be addressed.

DEVELOP

This phase involves implementing every viable idea for improving the business. The model requires that you continually look for changes that will lead to enhanced results in all areas of the business.

Within the DEVELOP phase, the actual turnaround work is completed. The **Universal Turnaround Model,** as depicted below, was the guide for you, a substitute for the experience that you now have. Here is a quick review.

UNIVERSAL TURNAROUND MODEL

The six steps are as follows:

- Assessing the situation
- Planning the turnaround project
- Improving cash management
- Reducing expenses
- Increasing revenue
- Monitoring and reassessing the situation

The steps are not complete without the resources that are outlined in the center of the model:

- **Accounting Information**
- **Industry Data**
- **Advisory Group**

During the last 30 days you used each of these resources in every step.

The DEVELOP phase involves developing work plans and then following them. It is developing results based on the plans generated to address problems discovered in the first step. You are obtaining a better sense of what is happening inside the business—what works and what doesn't work.

DOCUMENT

As you reflect on the overall experience, consider what you learned that can help you with your next turnaround project. Documentation is the focus of the rest of this chapter.

Turnaround Project Learning Points

In Chapter Two—Setting up the Project—the **Universal Project Management Model** was explained in detail. A project has three phases with action steps within each phase. The actual 30-day turnaround period is in the DEVELOP phase. This phase is hectic, frustrating and exciting all at the same time. Now, it is time to reflect on what happened, not necessarily from the business's point of view, but from your own. This experience should have moved you up the learning curve.

Now, the turnaround project is over. You can breathe a sigh of relief and perhaps celebrate the project's success and your own survival through it. Celebration is worthwhile. So is reflection.

The process is not complete until the learning points are documented. This prevents you, in subsequent months, quarters and years, from wasting money on what you have tried before with no success. Lessons should be learned once, not over and over again. Great documentation means there is no need to remember every detail.

For example, some of the **Universal Turnaround Model** steps might have been more impactful for you. Write that down so you can remember it in the future. If something didn't work, write that down too. Then develop your own model. Document everything that is worthwhile.

The *hows* of documentation

You might want to write your findings in a journal of some sort, or perhaps keep a database or software program like *Microsoft OneNote*. But, it doesn't necessarily matter *where* you document the learning points, just that you do it.

Learning Points for Project Management

The next page provides a sample worksheet for turnaround project documentation. It will give you an idea of what you can use to document turnaround learning points. It doesn't have to be long, but it must be done. If this form doesn't appeal to you, design your own.

You would be well advised to review Chapter Two on setting up projects to compare what you were thinking as the project began to what you are thinking now. Did the project design change? How is your relationship with the owner now versus when you first started the project? Would you work with him again?

In other words, this documents your major learning points from working on the turnaround projects.

PERSONAL LEARNING POINTS
BUSINESS TURNAROUND PROJECT

Learning Points	Comments and Observations
Being a Profit Expert	
Setting up the project	
Assessing the situation	
Planning the turnaround project	
Improving cash management	
Reducing expenses	
Increasing revenue	
Reassessing the situation	

Learning points for your accounting practice

The focus here is not the turnaround project per se. It is how the turnaround work affected you and your own accounting practice. Documenting what you learned about your own development as an accountant or *Profit Expert* is also critical.

Chapter One described what a Profit Expert does, the issues he faces, and what is needed in his Profit Expert's tool box. Did you like the work? Did the experience help you gain expertise?

Here are some other examples: The written agreement between you and the business owner stated that you would work with the business as a consultant for one year. Is that agreement still working? Are you communicating with the owner? How would you change the written agreement knowing what you know now? How will your accounting practice change now that you have completed the turnaround project?

There is much you have learned about being a Profit Expert that you should document. Written documentation clears the memory for more information.

The following worksheet allows you to capture the major learning points you have learned about yourself and your accounting practice. This is not about the turnaround project but about you and what you learned about project management, working with clients in troubled situations, etc!

PERSONAL LEARNING POINTS
ACCOUNTING PRACTICE/BEING A PROFIT EXPERT

Learning Points	Comments and Observations
Being a Profit Expert	
Personal business issues	
Technical business issues	
Relationship skills	
Project management	
Accounting practice management	
Other learning points	

Frequently Asked Questions

Will the success of the turnaround project lead to more work?

Yes, you already have a one-year agreement with the business owner. This should allow you to work with the business for at least several more months.

Word-of-mouth advertising and networking helps other owners of troubled small businesses find you. They need you and your turnaround expertise!

Remember the two major questions posed in Chapter Two, Setting up the Project, which I am asked often. Those questions are now easier to answer:

Can you help a small business in trouble? And what would you do with a small business with problems?

Now you know the answer. **ABSOLUTELY, you can help them!** You have done it at least once; you can do it again. Next time you can refine and enhance the models and processes used from *Red to Black in 30 Days* to be even more effective.

How are you compensated for your work?

I've suggested possible options for compensation throughout the book. My preferred option is a monthly fee or percentage of the new profits (maybe 20%-25%), whichever is greater.

And the third question: *How should your relationship with the business owner be formalized?*

A written agreement is always best. As illustrated in previous chapters, the turnaround work is too difficult, involved and volatile in nature not to have a written agreement between you and the business owner. A written agreement reminds everyone what is important and how business decisions are made.

SUMMARY—WHERE YOU SHOULD BE AT THIS POINT

You have concluded the 30-day turnaround project and have hopefully reached the identified outcomes. The business might not be totally stabilized and profitable but you, as the Profit Expert have provided profitable guidance throughout the 30 days and the business has greatly improved because of it. As the business accountant you have completed exactly what you committed to do in your initial letter of agreement and more.

You have a good sense of how the business should function, thus enabling you to continue working with the client as established in the original written agreement.

You analyzed the project from start to finish and documented the major learning points for future reference. The next project should run more smoothly than this one.

You developed expertise about project management generally and about turnaround projects specifically. You improved your ability to determine and design an effective scope of work. You determined compensation models that meet your needs.

Your management and Profit Expert skills are greatly enhanced. You gained wisdom that will help you advance your own practice in profit and stature.

You also developed a resource base, specifically advisors who can help you in future projects when needed. You know more now that accounting information is critical in small business success.

CHAPTER NINE
IT'S WORKING. NOW YOU ARE AN EXPERT!
Key Learning Points

- All models and processes presented in the book work:

  The **Universal Project Management Model** provides a foundation of continual improvement for any project. The model also is a guide for building the relationships needed to manage turnaround projects from beginning to end.

  The **Universal Turnaround Model** provides six action steps necessary in making troubled small businesses profitable. No troubled small business is totally out of the woods in 30 days; however, it can improve and stabilize. An Advisory Group is effective in providing guidance and counsel during the turnaround process.

  The **Universal Score Card** is an efficient and effective monitoring tool. It measures key business indicators on a weekly basis.

- Documentation is key here. Write down the major learning points that you acquired during this turnaround project. You only want to learn lessons once. Learning points should be captured on paper or digitally.

- Every small business needs a Profit Expert. You are that Profit Expert for this business and can be for others. You can rely on your own skills and not on someone else's to help businesses return to profitability.

    And most important of all, you have proved to yourself and others that you can perform valuable turnaround work. Congratulations again!

CASE I
Miriam's Art and Frame Shop—after the fact

Miriam is happy! Her shop is doing well, or at least better than it was before you were involved in the intricate workings of the business. Your time commitment is 3 to 4 hours per week reviewing the Score Card and financial statements together with Miriam and the new office manager you hired.

You continue to show great commitment to the company's success. You draw 20% of the profit each month and keep a pulse on the back office. You still watch and approve cash outlays, monitor expenses, and check margins to ensure that all products and services are profitable.

Miriam's Art and Frame shop did indeed survive. This business fit our criteria perfectly as small and capable of turning around quickly if the right changes and adjustments are made.

You are ready for a new challenge—another business to help turn around.

CASE II
Knecht's Roofing and Construction—after the fact

Knecht's Roofing and Construction is still in business. That marks a success right there. Kevin wouldn't be in business today if it hadn't been for your counsel and advice. Your relationship with Kevin was rocky at times, especially when you told him not to take a draw for a few weeks. That wasn't really business advice but personal financial advice.

The margin problem that perplexed Kevin was only solved by your focused analysis. It was difficult making Kevin understand that he could be more profitable winning fewer bids. But, that was indeed the case. Past losses were due to low bids, and winning all bids was not necessarily good.

All issues were addressed but not all resolved. Profitability remains tenuous. Your relationship with Kevin is intact and you are ready for the next phase in the turnaround process. He is not out of the woods yet, however.

CASE III
Sherwood's SureSave and Audio Alternatives— after the fact.

The central issue with Sherwood's business was not internal accounting per se, but rather external marketing. You were able to organize a great Advisory Group and make recommendations that helped create a new, profitable business model.

The relationship and project were successful.

This business provides good experience for any accountant working in turnaround situations. This expands the expertise of any accountant into areas where he might not have had much expertise— marketing and further business expansion. The business had to change because of competitive influences.

As the accountant, you were the expert in this situation. The marketing tools provided here were effective and easy to use.

You were paid appropriately for the work you successfully completed and are still connected with Sherwood's as an accountant and marketing consultant.